# COOK JAMAICAN!

## JOAN JACQUELINE LUE

Copyright © 2013 Joan Jacqueline Lue
All rights reserved.

ISBN: 1460916468
ISBN 13: 9781460916469

www.letscookjamican.com

THIS BOOK IS DEDICATED
TO MY MOTHER
CARMEN

# TABLE OF CONTENTS

INTRODUCTION · · · · · · · · · · · · · · · · · · · · · · · · · · · · · · · · · · · · · · · · · · · · · · · · · · · · · · · VII

WEIGHT AND MEASUREMENTS · · · · · · · · · · · · · · · · · · · · · · · · · · · · · · · · · · VIII

NOTES AND TIPS · · · · · · · · · · · · · · · · · · · · · · · · · · · · · · · · · · · · · · · · · · · · · · · IX

GLOSSARY OF FRUITS AND VEGETABLES · · · · · · · · · · · · · · · · · · · · · XI

RECIPES · · · · · · · · · · · · · · · · · · · · · · · · · · · · · · · · · · · · · · · · · · · · · · · · · · · · · · · XXIII

APPETIZERS · · · · · · · · · · · · · · · · · · · · · · · · · · · · · · · · · · · · · · · · · · · · · · · · · · · · · 1

SOUPS · · · · · · · · · · · · · · · · · · · · · · · · · · · · · · · · · · · · · · · · · · · · · · · · · · · · · · · · · · 17

MAIN DISHES · · · · · · · · · · · · · · · · · · · · · · · · · · · · · · · · · · · · · · · · · · · · · · · · · · 29

SIDE DISHES · · · · · · · · · · · · · · · · · · · · · · · · · · · · · · · · · · · · · · · · · · · · · · · · · · · · 51

SWEETS AND DESSERTS · · · · · · · · · · · · · · · · · · · · · · · · · · · · · · · · · · · · · · 61

DRINKS · · · · · · · · · · · · · · · · · · · · · · · · · · · · · · · · · · · · · · · · · · · · · · · · · · · · · · · · · 81

JAMS JELLIES PRESERVES · · · · · · · · · · · · · · · · · · · · · · · · · · · · · · · · · · · · 97

ACKNOWLEDGEMENTS · · · · · · · · · · · · · · · · · · · · · · · · · · · · · · · · · · · · · · · 109

# INTRODUCTION

In this small book, I wish to share with you the pleasure of Jamaican cooking. Whether you are a foreigner who is curious about this aspect of our culture, a second or third-generation Jamaican living in the USA, Canada or Britain, or a Jamaican who wants to have a guideline for the basics, this book will provide you with an overview of the island's cuisine. Many of the recipes are traditional favourites that are close to every Jamaican's heart, for example Mackerel Rundown, Rice and Peas or Grater Cake. In others, imaginative use is made of our indigenous products such as in Callaloo Tartlets or Ham with Mango-Ginger Sauce. In all of the recipes, one will experience the flavours, aromas and textures of a Jamaican kitchen.

My only hope is that the reader will enjoy these recipes as much as I have enjoyed writing them. Happy cooking.

Visit www.letscookjamican.com

# WEIGHT AND MEASUREMENTS

| | | |
|---|---|---|
| 3 teaspoons | equals | 1 tablespoon |
| 4 tablespoon | " | ¼ cup |
| 8 ozs. | " | 1 cup |
| 2 cups | " | 1 pint |
| 2 pints | " | 1 quart |
| 4 quarts | " | 1 gallon |
| 1 lb | " | 16 ozs. |

## METRIC CONVERSION

| | | |
|---|---|---|
| 454 grams | equals | 1 lb. |
| 1 kilogram | " | 2 lbs. 3 ozs |
| 1 liter | " | 1 quart 2 ozs. |
| 250 ml | " | 8 ½ ozs |
| 2 ½ cm | " | 1 inch |
| 30 ½ cm | " | 1 foot |

## EQUIVALENTS

| | | |
|---|---|---|
| 1 lb. sugar | equals | 2 cups |
| 1 lb. flour | " | 4 cups |
| 1 lb. butter or margarine | " | 2 cups |
| 1 lb. rice" | " | 2 ¼ cups |
| 1 lb. cornmeal | " | 3 cups |
| 1 lb. raisins | " | 3 cups |

# NOTES AND TIPS

The best ingredients to use are fresh ingredients. As a general rule, don't ever scrimp on the quality of meat, fish or produce for satisfying, healthy results. When called for in this book, use freshly grated nutmeg and fresh garlic. When fresh thyme is not available using dried will give a very close result. When fresh Scotch Bonnet peppers, a cornerstone of Jamaican cooking, are not available, there is a variety of pepper sauces and crushed pepper available not only here but in overseas metropolitan markets. Use the rule of thumb that a medium pepper is roughly equal to 1 tablespoon bottled pepper sauce or crushed pepper.

The flavour and texture of fresh coconut juice is unmatchable, but if this isn't available, a 50 gram bag of coconut powder or a 5 oz. tin of unsweetened coconut cream can be used as a substitute for a medium coconut.

# GLOSSARY OF FRUITS AND VEGETABLES

**ACKEE** The national fruit of Jamaica. Originated in West Africa. Consists of a beautiful vibrant pink pod filled with normally three yellow arils each with a large shiny black seed. It is unsafe to eat the fruit unless the pod has opened naturally. Usually the seeds and inner pink membranes are removed from the arils, which are then boiled, drained and sautéed with salted cod fish to make the national dish. The tree is not formally cultivated and the fruit is sold by the dozen.

**AVOCADO** A Jamaican always refers to an avocado as simply a pear. Jamaicans are purists when it comes to this rich and delicate fruit, always eating it just peeled and sliced lengthwise. The prized variety is the Simmonds, which is large and heavy with a thick, shiny skin. Today avocados are grown all over the tropics, but originated in Mexico. They have a high fat content, but contain no cholesterol and are a nutritional powerhouse with potassium, vitamins B, C, E and K and folic acid. Jamaicans would sometimes eat pears as a substitute for butter, such as with bullas.

BANANA BLOSSOM WITH YOUNG BANANAS ON THE TREE

**BANANA** This fruit has been grown in tropical regions since antiquity. The tree has large elongated leaves and a large fibrous trunk with the fruit actually growing upside down in bunches. Usually, one tree will produce one bunch. After bearing, the parts above ground die and disappear. A new plant grows from suckers put out by the old plant. The banana was likely to have been brought here by the Spanish in the 1500's and did well in the fertile soil. Varieties grown today include the Gros Michel, the Robusta, the Lacatan and the Valery. For Jamaica, bananas are a very important export crop. In local cuisine, not only is the ripe banana enjoyed eaten fresh but in cakes, breads, fritters and fresh fruit punches. Green bananas are boiled and eaten hot as the starch in a meal or grated and made into porridge or dumplings and fried into chips. They are a good source of Vitamin B, C and potassium.

# GLOSSARY OF FRUITS AND VEGETABLES

**BREADFRUIT** Bears from a very attractive tree with large beautiful leaves. Originated in the Pacific islands and brought here by the infamous Captain Bligh in 1793. The breadfruit is a large ovoid fruit with a thick green skin and a fibrous heart. The starchy flesh varies from cream to yellow. Can be boiled, roasted or sliced and fried after being roasted. The blossoms, called swords, can also be preserved in sugar.

**CALLALOO** A spinach-like vegetable amaranth, species amaranthus dubius, found in the tropics and subtropics in India, Africa, Asia and the Caribbean. Callaloo is mineral-rich and contains iron along with vitamins A, B, C and K. It is served sautéed or steamed and in soups, rice dishes and patties.

**CASSAVA** comes from a hardy perennial shrub of either the bitter or sweet variety. Bitter cassava must be processed to remove prussic acid before being prepared. The tubers grow below ground with creamy white flesh and thick, rough brown skin. An important food source in Jamaica from pre-Columbian times, cassava is processed into flour and made into an unleavened bread called bammy or baked into pones and puddings.

**COCO** The plant produces a firm tuber with creamy white flesh and brown, hairy skin and large, heart-shaped leaves that are also edible. The tuber should be heavy for its size and should never be eaten raw. It is normally boiled in salted water or added to soups in Jamaica. The leaves are traditionally used to make Pepperpot Soup but as they become harder and harder to find in the market, callaloo can be used instead. Coco has been grown since ancient times in all the tropical areas of the world, and was eaten in pre-Columbian times by our indigenous people. Also called taro or dasheen.

**COCONUT** bears from the coconut palm which has been the called the "Tree of Life". The coconut at different stages is almost two different fruits. A young coconut has a green or yellowish exterior, a beige husk and a large, tough seed containing soft, semi-transparent jelly and a refreshing liquid called the "water". This water is healthy and completely sterile, containing B vitamins and electrolytes like potassium and calcium. It is a perfect hydrating fluid for a person who has lost fluid for any reason. After cutting through the husk and into the seed, the water is poured out, the coconut is split in two and the transparent to white jelly spooned out and enjoyed.

### COCONUT TREE

As the coconut matures, the exterior and husk turn brown, the seed hardens, the jelly thickens, hardens and turns pure white. The quantity of the water decreases and its taste deteriorates. At this point, when the flesh is removed from the shell with a sharp knife, there is a thin brown layer on the back. The flesh can now be grated, and mixed with water to extract a milky juice. This can be used in many culinary preparations and can be processed to yield a valuable oil.

The coconut has been grown since ancient times throughout the world's tropical regions.

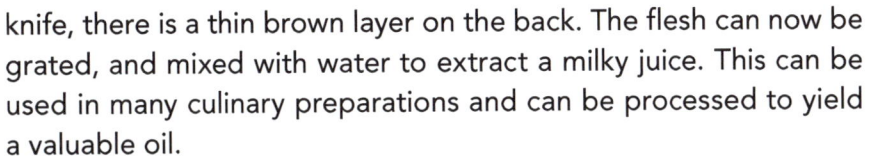

A JELLY COCONUT WITH THE REFRESHING WATER

**COFFEE** First grown in Ethiopia, coffee arrived in the Caribbean when seedlings were dispatched to Martinique from Paris by King Louis XV of France in 1723. Every coffee plant in Jamaica today is descended from a single seedling brought to Jamaica, probably from Martinique, in 1728, by former governor Lawes of Jamaica. This Arabica bean is strictly differentiated depending on where it is grown. At a height of 3500 to 5500 feet above sea level, it is Blue Mountain Coffee, at 1500 to 3000 feet it is High Mountain. Blue Mountain, considered to be the best in the world, is mellow and fragrant.

RIPE COFFEE BERRIES

**CUSTARD APPLE** A roundish or heart-shaped fruit with a rough skin, that is pale yellow with a pink blush when ripe. Inside is a creamy pulp with black seeds throughout and a fibrous core. Only mildly popular, the fruit is also called bull's heart. The tree grows wild and is not formally cultivated in Jamaica. Makes a good juice and ice cream.

**DASHEEN** A variety of coco. The name could be a corruption of the French "de chine" meaning "from China".

# GLOSSARY OF FRUITS AND VEGETABLES

**EDDOE** A small variety of the coco whose skin consists of a rough brown covering under which is a distinctive pink layer.

**GARDEN CHERRY** Also called acerola or West Indian cherry. Small, roundish, red fruit with a large three-part pit. Bears on a very attractive tree with smallish leaves and beautiful pink blossoms. The fruit has an exceptionally high level of Vitamin C and is very perishable. The flavour is sweet and delicate. Makes excellent juice, jams, jellies and sauces.

**GINGER** Grown since ancient times in Asia, it was one of the first spices to be introduced into Europe. This veritable wonder root has countless medicinal and gastronomic uses. It adds a spicy warmth to both sweet and savoury dishes and to refreshing and stimulating beverages. It was brought by the Spanish to Jamaica where it became an important export crop. Jamaican ginger is considered the best ginger in the world. Highly desired all over the world, its production is very labour-intensive as it has to be peeled by hand. The parishes of St. Anne, Manchester, Clarendon and Trelawny have the most ideal soil for ginger.

**GUAVA** A palm-sized round or pear-shaped fruit with an exquisite and powerful aroma and flavour. In Jamaica, guava, a member of the myrtle family, is not cultivated but grows in the wild. The thin skin ranges from green to light yellow. The flesh that is either light yellow or a beautiful pink forms a cup around a large pulpy mass of small light yellow seeds. This fruit is used in drinks, "cheese", jams and jellies, and pastry fillings. A very nutritious fruit containing iron, calcium, phosphorus, and vitamins A, B and C.

**GUINEP** Small fruit that grows in bunches with a green skin that can be popped open with the teeth and peeled away to reveal a soft, delicate creamy-peach pulp covering a large seed. The guinep, is related to the lychee and has a sweet, tart taste. Also called the mamoncillo.

**JUNE PLUM** Palm-sized oblong fruit that starts out green and turns golden yellow with a sweet-tart taste and a single spiky seed. Brought to Jamaica by Captain Blight from the South Seas in the late 1700's. Delicious peeled and eaten raw or in juices and jams.

# COOK JAMAICAN!

**MANGO** Delectable fruit originating in Asia that comes in many varieties, such as Bombay, East Indian, St. Julian, Hayden and the whimsical Sweetie Come Brush Mi. The tree is generally large and long-living, with long, slender leaves and tiny peach-coloured blossoms that grow in clusters. The fruit came to Jamaica in the mid-1700's. Mangoes have a thick skin, a large single seed and sweet, fragrant, rich-tasting flesh that is a vivid orange. They are a nutritional powerhouse containing not only vitamin C, but beta-carotene, vitamin A and the B vitamins. It is generally known that during mango season the nutritional index in children rises. The most highly prized mangoes have very little or no string. Ranges in size from 3" to 5" in diameter.

**NASEBERRY** A brown-coloured spherical fruit ranging from 2 to 4 inches across. There is a soft core surrounded by flat, black seeds in a star formation. The flesh is enclosed in a thin skin, is sweet and soft with a slightly gritty texture at the edges. When the trunk of the tree is cut latex gum flows. Native to Mexico and Central America. Also called the sapodilla. Belongs to the same family as the starapple.

**OTAHEITI APPLE** A pear-shaped fruit with a bright red skin, pure white delicately-flavoured flesh and a single brown seed nestled in the middle. The fruit bears from vivid fuchsia blossoms in bunches that grow close to the branches. The leaves tend to grow in a tent shape, with the blossoms and fruit always growing under the leaves. Because of this, Jamaicans will say a person is "as secretive as otaheiti apple".

OTAHEITI APPLE BLOSSOM

When juiced, the skin turns the juice a light pink. The darker the skin the sweeter the fruit will be. This fruit should never be peeled as much flavour, colour and nutrients are contained in the skin. Can be stewed or made into juice, chutneys, jellies and jams.

**ORTANIQUE** A hybrid of the orange and the tangerine developed, maybe accidentally, in Jamaica. The rind is a beautiful orange colour, the flesh is sweet and yields a high quantity of juice. The name combines the words orange, tangerine and unique. Use for juices, salads, cakes, jams and jellies.

# GLOSSARY OF FRUITS AND VEGETABLES

**PAPAYA** Called pawpaw in Jamaica. Succulent fruit that when cut reveals a brilliant orange flesh, that is soft, sweet and not at all sour with a profusion of small, round black seeds. Pawpaws range in size from up to 8 pounds to as small as 1 pound. The fruit is oval or pear-shaped and the skin and flesh contain the powerful enzyme papain. Because of this enzyme, fresh pawpaw can never be used in any recipe using gelatin, as it will prevent it from ever jelling. This same enzyme makes the pawpaw skin an effective meat-tenderizer. Papaya makes wonderful juices, milk shakes, fruit salads, jams and jellies.

**PIMENTO** This rich, complex spice is the dried unripe berries of the Pimenta dioica tree, a member of the myrtle family and resembles black peppercorns. In the Jamaican countryside, large stone squares or oblongs, called barbeques, can still be seen. These are used for drying the berries and date from the 1800's. Pimento is also called "allspice" outside of Jamaica, because the flavour and aroma is reminiscent of a combination of cloves, nutmeg and cinnamon. Native to Mexico, the Greater Antilles, and Central America. Pimento is the distinctive flavour in jerk, and is wonderful in sorrel drinks, makes a liqueur called dram, is used in cakes, puddings, soups, sauces, chutneys and meat dishes.

**PINEAPPLE PLANT**

**PINEAPPLE** This delicious fruit originated in Paraguay and Brazil, spread upwards through South and Central America and the Caribbean. With a thick yellow, greenish or reddish skin and a crown of straight spiky leaves, this is actually a multiple fruit, as each pineapple is actually many flowers spirally arranged that press together and then end up growing as one "fruit". The flesh ranges from pale to bright yellow with a fibrous core. The flavour is sweet, tangy and exquisite. The English successfully grew the pineapple in greenhouses, the very first one being presented to King James II. It was so prized that even the fibrous core was eaten. Taken by the Spanish invaders first back to Europe, then to the Phillipines, where it thrived. In the English-speaking Caribbean, the pineapple came to be a symbol of welcome.

**PLANTAIN** A member of the banana family. Has a thicker skin and heavier and coarser flesh than the banana. Plantains are never eaten raw but are always either boiled, fried, baked, or made into tarts. A common side dish in Jamaican cuisine.

**PUMPKIN** The variety of pumpkin grown and used in Jamaica is the Calabaza. A medium-sized pumpkin ranging from six to twelve pounds, having a creamy skin striated with dark green. The bright orange flesh is thick and dense. When a whole pumpkin is cut, inexplicably, beads of moisture appear on the cut surface. So, when a Jamaican says, "You a go fine out how water walk go a pumpkin belly.", he means you are going to find out something you would rather not know.

**SCOTCH BONNET PEPPER** This small brightly-coloured pepper imparts the distinctive flavour to Jamaican cooking. The species of hot pepper called Capsicum chinense turns from green to yellow to orange-red as it ripens. Avoid touching the seeds and ribs with your fingers but if you do get burnt, rub the affected spot with sugar or oil, instead of washing with water.

**SORREL** is the rosy-red sepals that grow on a shrub called hibiscus sabdariffa, that is a member of the hibiscus family. At first yellow flowers bloom on the shrub then fall off. The sepals grow from where the blossoms fell. They are harvested as the Christmas season gets underway and can be seen in large piles or in plastic bags in the market. Jamaicans love making the sorrel into a refreshing drink but it can also be made into jams, jellies and preserves. On a visit to any Jamaican home during the holidays, most certainly you will be offered a glass of sorrel and a slice of Christmas fruitcake. Sorrel is high in Vitamin C. In other tropical areas sorrel is called flor de Jamaica and roselle.

## GLOSSARY OF FRUITS AND VEGETABLES

**SOURSOP** A large fruit with a thick, green rough skin that peels away easily to reveal a whitish pulp with large black seeds throughout and a fibrous core. The flavour is at the same time slightly tangy and creamy. Makes an excellent nectar prepared either with condensed milk and nutmeg or sugar and lime juice. Good also in ice cream. Soursop is called guanabana in the Spanish-speaking Caribbean.

**STARAPPLE** Round fruit either green or purple in colour with a thick inedible rind. Inside are soft gelatinous segments holding flat, black seeds surrounded by sweet, creamy pulp. When cut crosswise, the seeds have a star formation, hence the name. There is a detectable difference in flavour between the green and purple varieties. Starapples are mainly eaten fresh or combined with oranges and condensed milk to make matrimony. Because the starapple doesn't ever fall from the tree no matter how ripe it is, Jamaicans will say derisively about a stingy person, "Him mean like starapple."

**SUGARCANE** This tall, graceful plant is actually a grass, that originated in the South Pacific, and ended travelling to all tropical regions of the world. Sugarcane was grown and sugar produced in India as long as 5000 years ago. Growing to anywhere from 6 to14 feet, sugarcane has a stalk topped by elongated green leaves. The thick, jointed stalk is rich in the juice that is boiled down to eventually produce sugar. The stalks can be peeled and cut into small sticks and eaten fresh and the chilled juice can be enjoyed. Fresh cane juice is an aid to digestion. Molasses, wet sugar and rum are other products of sugarcane. Cane contains calcium and iron.

Sugarcane had profound impact on the economic, social and cultural history of the Caribbean. It was, literally, the oil that ran the financial machine of the region from the 15th to the 19th century. The expression, 'as rich as a West Indian planter' came into being. Sugar wealth was conspicuous for all to see back in Britain, in the form of buildings and structures. Generally, Britishers owned and ran the plantations. As raising cane was labour intensive, it led to the importation of African slaves, then after Emancipation, labourers from India and Asia were enticed to come and work in the canefields. Today, the descendants of all of these people, in large part, make up Jamaica's population.

PEELED SUGARCANE

**SWEET SOP** Roundish, green-coloured fruit covered in bumps with a fibrous core and cream-coloured flesh with small black seeds throughout. The flesh is sweet, creamy, and a little gritty towards the edges. Makes excellent juice and ice cream. High in iron.

**TAMARIND** Long, brown beanpod-shaped fruit with a brittle outer shell and a pulp-covered seeds. Has a strong tangy flavour. Jamaican children love "tambrin balls", little globes of tamarind fruit and sugar. Native to Africa since ancient times. Has spread to most tropical areas of the world. Used for drinks, sauces, sweets. High in Vitamin C.

TAMARIND

# GLOSSARY OF FRUITS AND VEGETABLES

**PIECES OF CUT YAM**

**YAM** Nutritious tuber of which there are many varieties. Not to be confused with the sweet potato. They grow from a perennial vine and are rich in fiber, vitamins and minerals. Yams have a rough, thick brown skin and depending on the variety the flesh can be white, cream, or yellow. Yam must be cooked as there are toxins present in its raw state and handling the raw flesh may cause irritation in the form of itching. If this happens, wash the affected area under cold running water. Varieties available in Jamaica include Yellow, White, St. Vincent, Renta, and Sweet.

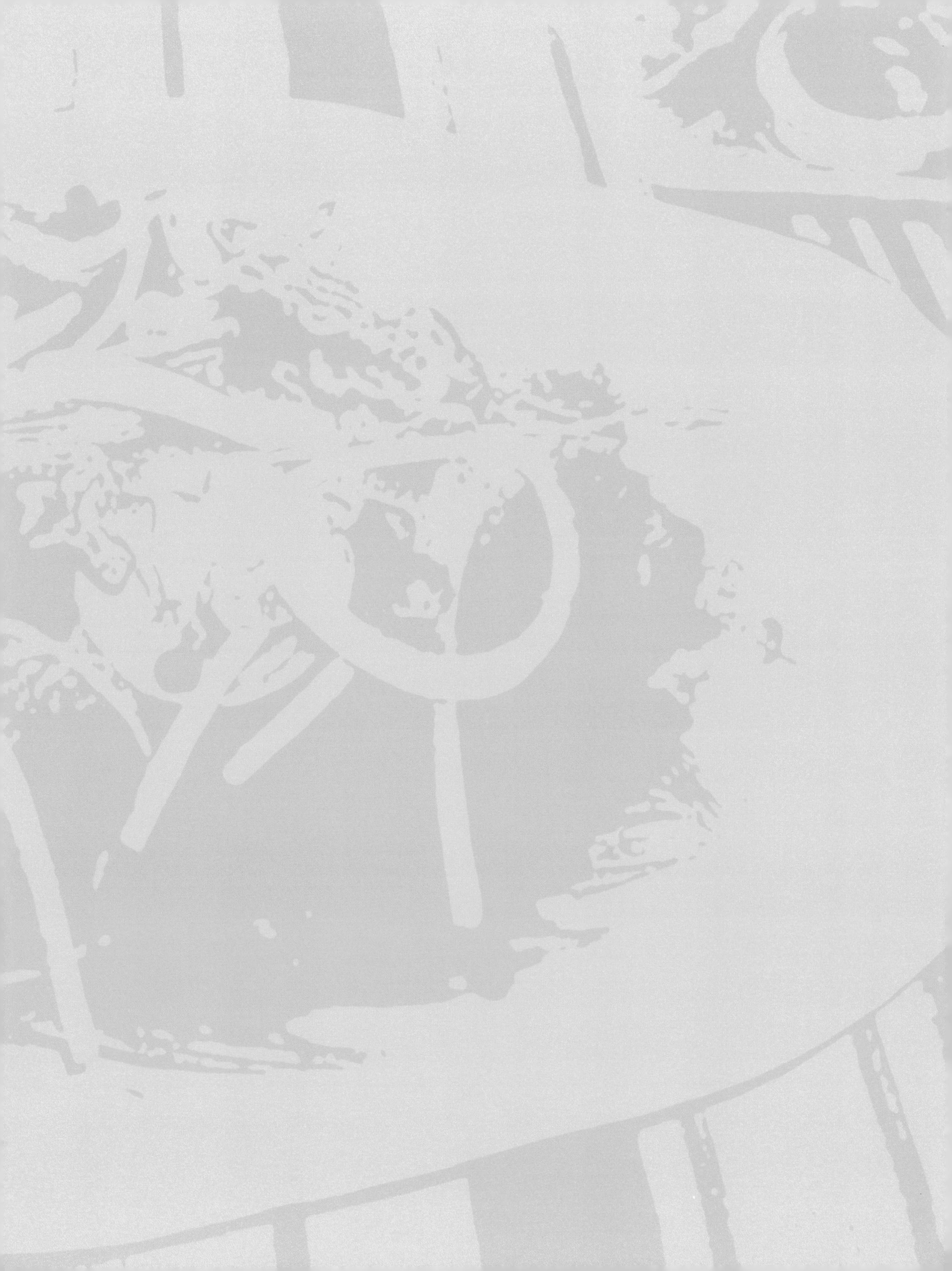

# RECIPES

## APPETIZERS

- Ackee Boats
- Callaloo Tartlets
- Stamp and Go
- Pepper Shrimps
- Pick-up Saltfish
- Cheese Dip with Plantain Chips
- Smoked Marlin Bites
- Beef Patties
- Patty Dough
- Shortcrust Pastry

## SOUPS

- Pumpkin Beef Soup
- Chicken Soup
- Red Peas Soup
- Pepperpot Soup
- Gungo Peas Soup
- Fish Tea
- Mannish Water

## MAIN DISHES

- Ackee and Saltfish
- Escoveitched Fish
- Mackerel Rundown
- Chicken Fricasee
- Jerked Pork
- Jerked Chicken
- Roasted Ham
- Curried Goat
- Curried Shrimps
- Lobstertails in Butter Sauce
- Oxtail
- Roast Beef
- Stewed Peas

## SIDE DISHES

- Rice and Peas
- Festival
- Yam Souffle
- Sweet Potato Casserole
- Fried Bammy
- Fried Dumplings

## SWEETS AND DESSERTS

- Coconut Bread
- Banana Bread
- Gizzardas "Pinch-Me-Round"
- Rum Trifle
- Sweet Potato Pudding
- Fruit Salad
- Matrimony
- Otaheiti Apple Pie
- Grater Cake
- Bullas
- Plantain Tarts
- Christmas Fruitcake

## BEVERAGES

- Ginger Beer
- Sorrel
- Shandy
- Blue Mountain Coffee Float
- Pina Colada
- Rum Punch
- Mango limeade
- Soursop juice
- Lime squash
- Planters Punch
- Daiquiri
- Simple Syrup

## JAM JELLIES AND PRESERVES

- Otaheiti Apple Chutney
- Ortanique Jelly
- Sorrel Preserves
- June Plum Jam
- Pineapple Chutney
- Stewed Guavas
- Orange Pepper Jelly

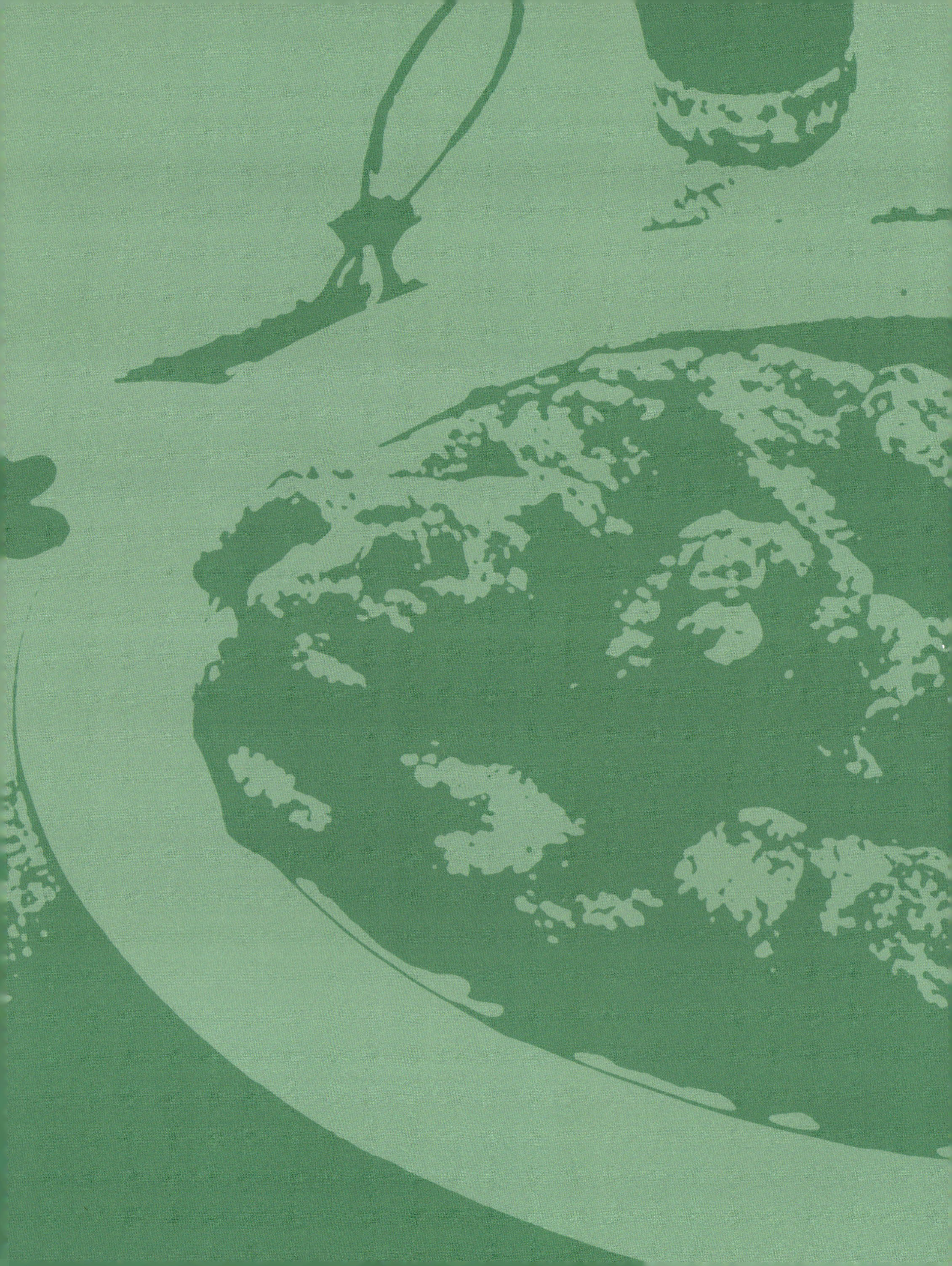

# APPETIZERS

## APPETIZERS

# ACKEE BOATS

**SHORTCRUST PASTRY (P 15)**

**ACKEE AND SALTFISH (P 29)**
8 ozs.　　　　　Cheese　　　　　　　　　　225 g.

Use either Cheddar, Gouda or Swiss. cheese, or any combination of two or three of them. Grate coarsely and set aside.

Roll out Shortcrust Pastry on a floured board to a 1/8 inch/2mm thickness. Cut and fit dough into small round, oval or boat-shaped tins. Prick with a fork. Chill the tins for 30 minutes. Bake in preheated 350°F oven for about 12-15 minutes. Remove from oven and fill each tartlet with about 2 tablespoons of Ackee and Saltfish. Sprinkle grated cheese over ackee and return to oven for about 5 minutes. Serve hot.

Makes about 24

# CALLALOO TARTLETS

Spinach can be substituted for the callaloo. Omit the addition of water during cooking and leave skillet uncovered.

| | | |
|---|---|---|
| 4 ozs. | Salted Codfish | 120 grams |
| 1 lb | Callaloo | 450 grams |
| 1 large | Onion | 1 large |
| 1 large stalk | Scallion | 1 large stalk |
| ½ tsp | Scotch Bonnet Pepper | ½ tsp. |
| ½ tsp | Thyme | ½ tsp |
| 2 tbsp | Oil | 2 tbsp |
| 2 | Eggs | 2 |
| 1 cup | Milk | 250 ml |
| 1 cup | Cheese (grated) | 250 ml |
| | Shortcrust Pastry (P 15) | |

Soak fish in enough cold water to cover for 2 hours. Remove all skin, scales, bone and fins. Flake and set aside.

Make Shortcrust Pastry. Roll out to 1/8"/2mm thickness and cut in 3"/5cm circles. Line muffin or tartlet tins with circles and leave to chill in the fridge for about 30 minutes.

Wash callaloo carefully under cold running water. Roll the leaves together tightly and slice thinly through leaves and stems. Slice onion and scallion thinly, chop pepper. Pour oil in large skillet and place on high heat. Saute onion, scallion, pepper and codfish stirring occasionally until onion is slightly browned then add callaloo and thyme. Add 1/3 cup /90 ml of water to pot, cover and lower heat to medium and simmer for about 20 minutes. Cool.

Grate cheese coarsely. Preheat oven to 400°F.

Fill each tart shell with about 2 tablespoons of callaloo filling and top with about a teaspoonful of cheese. Place in preheated oven for about 15 minutes or until cheese is bubbly. Serve hot.

APPETIZERS

# STAMP AND GO

No one really knows how these fritters got their name, but I suspect that it's because once the batter is laid down in the oil or "stamped", they are ready quickly.

| | | |
|---|---|---|
| 1 lb | All-purpose flour | 450 g |
| 2 tsp. | Salt | 2 tsp. |
| | Ice cold water | |
| 2 stalks | Scallion | 2 stalks |
| 1 | Scotch Bonnet pepper | 1 |
| | or | |
| 1 tbsp | Pepper Sauce | 1 tbsp |
| ½ lb | Salted Codfish | 225 g |
| | Cooking Oil | |

Soak fish in enough cold water to cover for 3 hours. Remove all bones, skin, scales and fins. Flake and set aside. Peel and slice scallion thinly. Remove seeds from pepper, if used, and chop finely.

Into a large bowl, sift flour once and add salt, scallion, pepper or pepper sauce and flaked fish. Add about 2 cups/500 ml iced water and stir well.

In a heavy skillet pour cooking oil to a depth of about ½ inch/1 cm.

Over medium-high burner, heat oil till tiny ripples are seen on the top. Drop batter by the tablespoonful into oil and fry on both sides till golden brown. Drain on absorbent towels or brown paper. Serve hot.

Makes about 60 fritters.

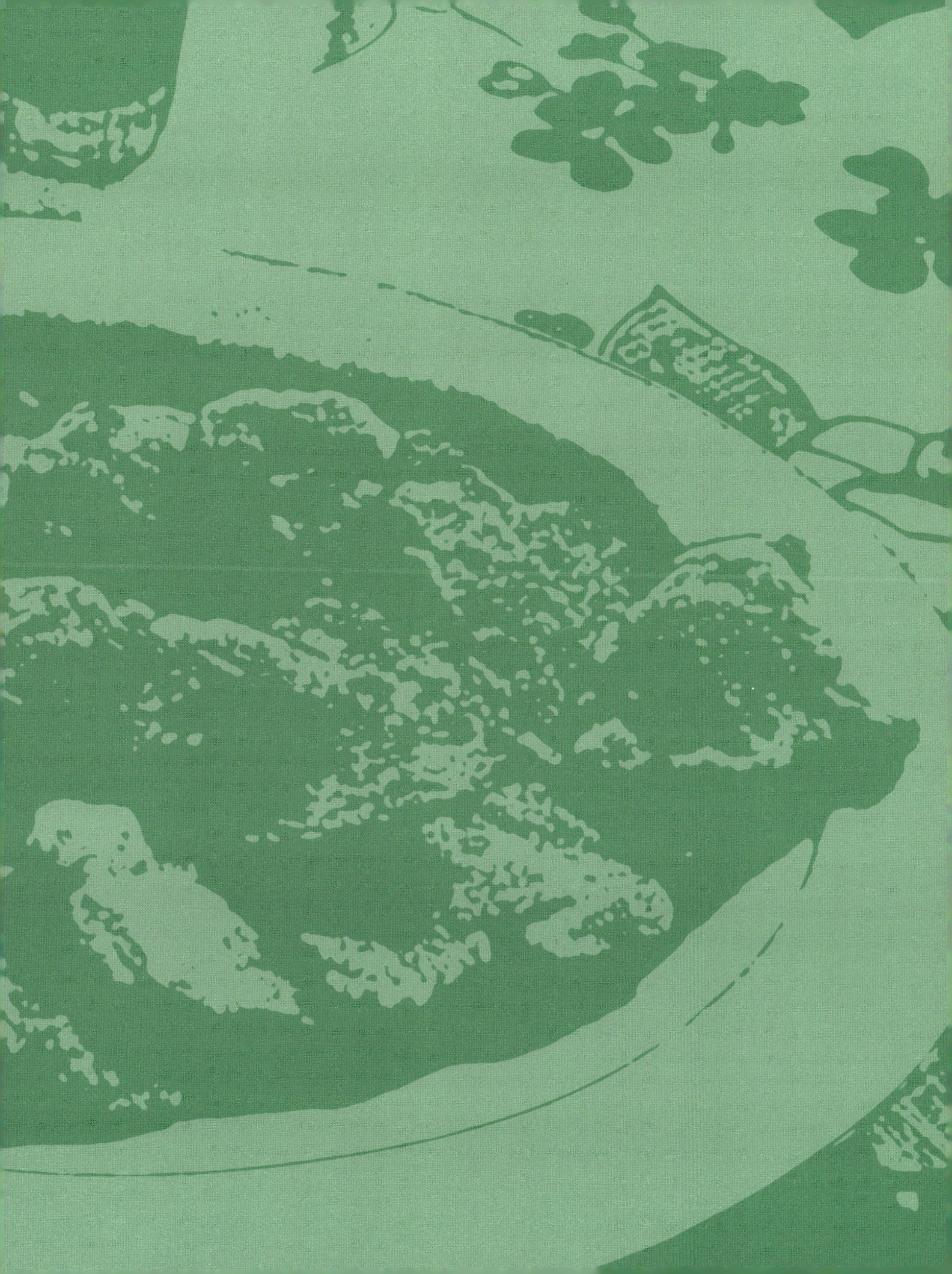

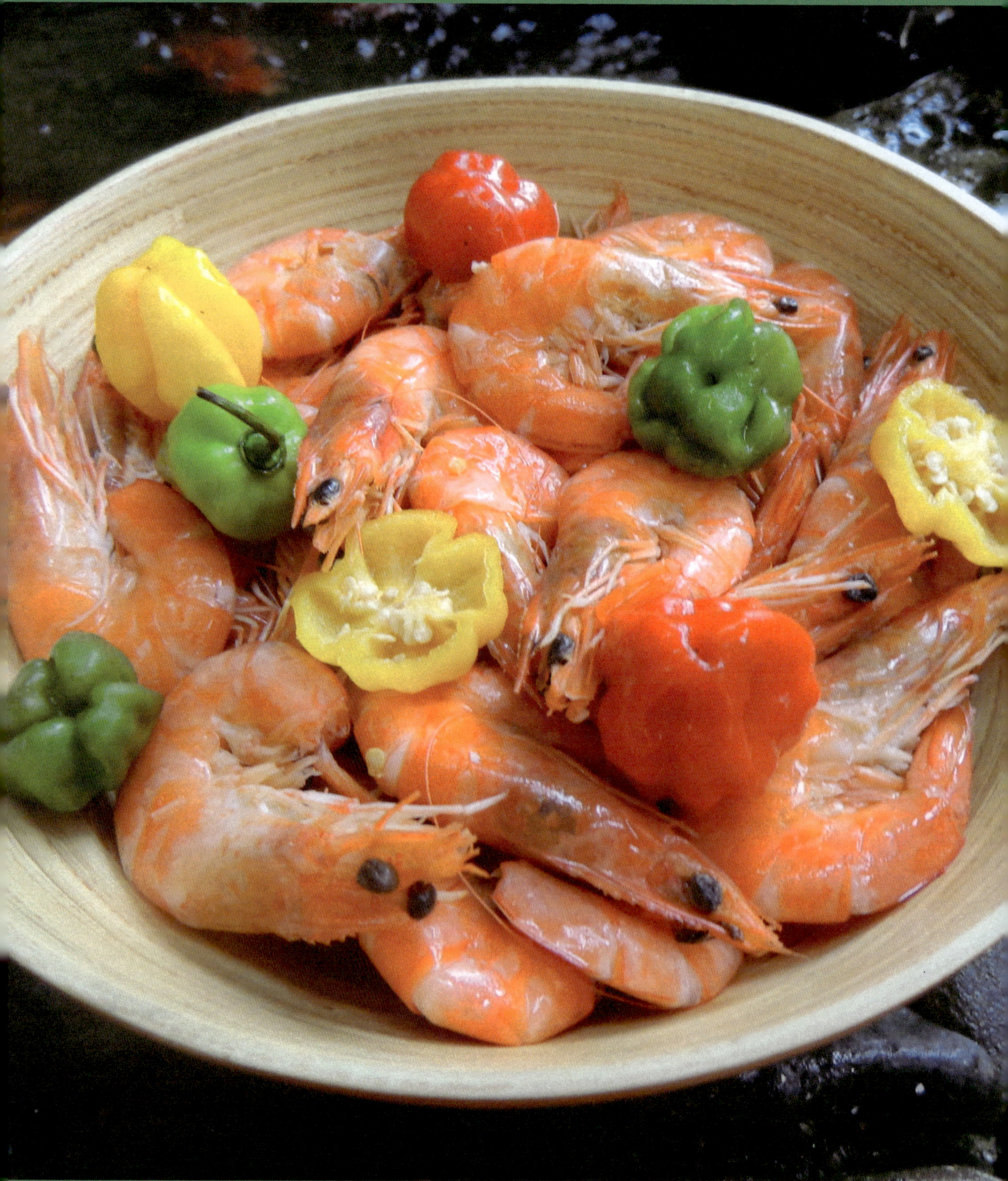

# PEPPER SHRIMPS

Middle Quarters, a town in the parish of St. Elizabeth, situated near the Black River is famous for this delicacy. Vendors sell the shrimp by small bagfuls.

| | | |
|---|---|---|
| 1 lb | River crayfish or whole shrimp | 450 grams |
| 4 cups | Water | 1 liter |
| 2 level tbsp | Salt | 2 level tbsp |
| 4 | Scotch Bonnet Peppers | 4 |

In a medium-sized saucepan, bring water and salt to boil. Chop peppers coarsely. Rinse crayfish or shrimp thoroughly under cold running water, leaving heads and shells on. Add to boiling water along with Scotch Bonnet Pepper. Cook uncovered for 15 minutes. Remove pan from fire and drain liquid. Allow pieces of pepper to remain on the crayfish. Serve at room temperature with shells and head still intact.

Serves 4-6

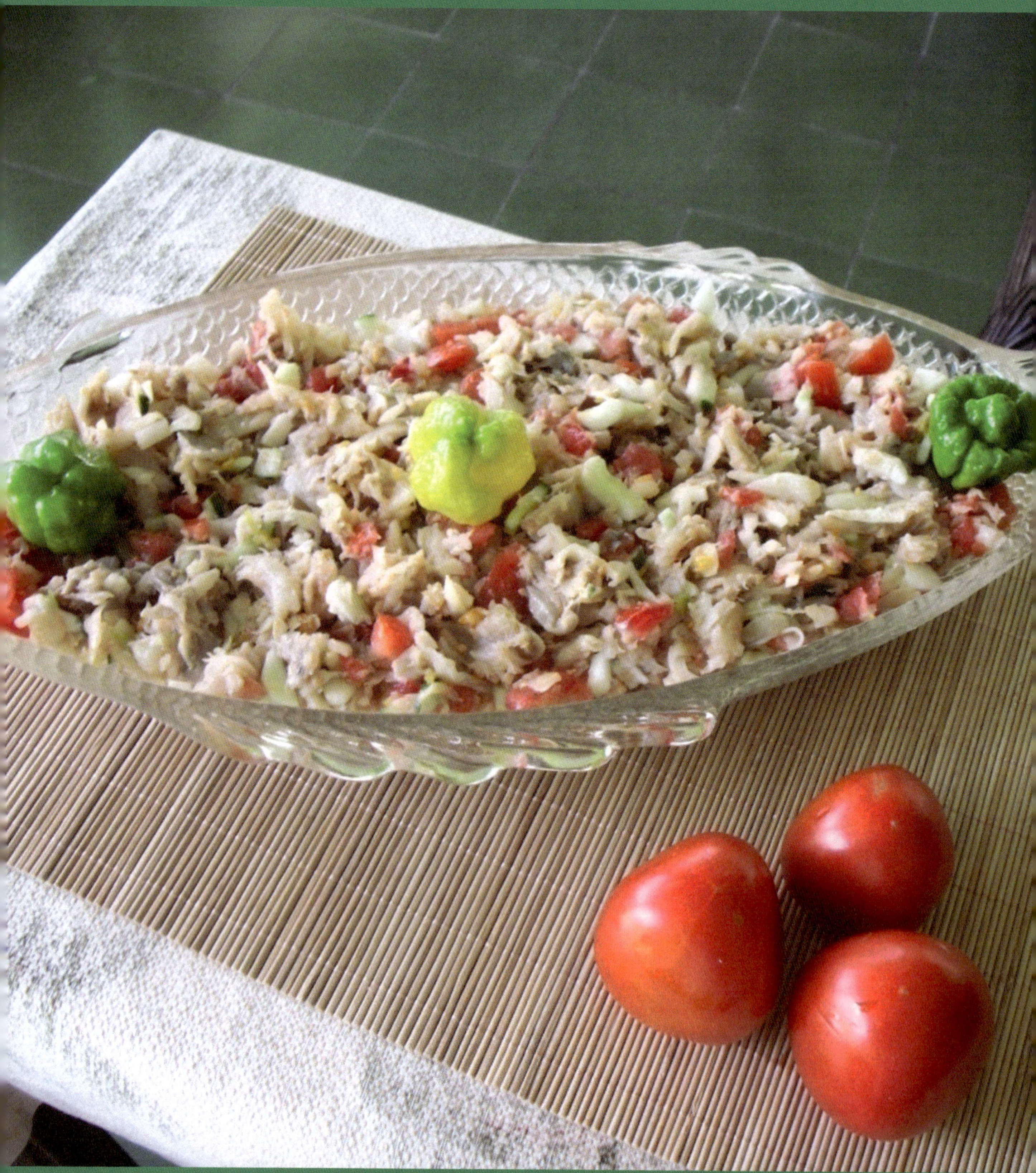

# PICK-UP SALTFISH

| | | |
|---|---|---|
| 1 lb. | Saltfish | 450 g |
| 1 | Small Cucumber | 1 |
| 1 | Large Onion | 1 |
| 1 | Large Tomato | 1 |
| 1 | Scotch Bonnet Pepper | 1 |
| | or | |
| 1 tbsp | Bottled Crushed Pepper | 1 tbsp |
| ½ cup | White Vinegar | 125 ml |
| ¼ cup | Coconut Oil | 60 ml |
| 1 tbsp | Sesame Seed Oil | 1 tbsp |

Wash and soak fish in enough cold water to cover for 3 hours. Remove scales, skin, bones and fins. Flake fish and place in bowl. Peel away strips of skin from the cucumber at even intervals all around, cut lengthwise in quarters, remove seeds, then slice each quarter thinly. Dice onion and fresh pepper finely, if it's being used. Dice tomato. Add cucumber, onion, fresh or crushed pepper and tomato to fish. Then add vinegar, coconut oil and sesame oil. Combine well. Allow to rest for at least 3–4 hours in the refrigerator. Serve at room temperature with water crackers.

Serves 6–8.

In Jamaica, this dish is often eaten with "water crackers", hard round crackers. If unavailable, use any firm unsalted cracker.

APPETIZERS

# CHEESE DIP WITH PLANTAIN CHIPS

| | | |
|---|---|---|
| 1 lb | Cheese | 450 g |
| 8 ozs. | Sour Cream | 225 g. |
| 2 cloves | Garlic | 2 cloves |
| 1 stalk | Scallion | 1 stalk |
| 1 tsp | Hot Pepper Sauce | 1 tsp |
| ½ tsp | Mustard | ½ tsp |
| 1 tbsp | White wine vinegar | 1 tbsp |
| 2 ozs. | Cashews | 60 g |
| 3 | Green Plantains | 3 |
| | Oil for frying | |

Use Cheddar or Edam cheese. Grate on the fine side of the grater. In medium bowl, combine with sour cream, minced garlic, finely chopped scallion, hot pepper sauce, mustard and vinegar. Beat with an electric mixer on low speed or mix very well by hand. Reserve 6 or 7 whole cashews for garnish and chop the rest coarsely. Add the chopped nuts to cheese mixture. Pile into a decorative bowl and garnish with whole nuts and a small sprig of parsley. Chill until ready to serve.

### PLANTAIN CHIPS

Peel plantains and slice thinly. Heat oil in large skillet until you can see small ripples in the top. Add slices and fry until golden on each side. Drain on absorbent paper. Serve with cheese dip.

# SMOKED MARLIN BITES

| | | |
|---|---|---|
| 4 ozs. | Smoked Marlin | 120 g. |
| 3 ozs. | Cream Cheese (softened) | 90 g. |
| 1 tbsp | Chopped Chives | 1 tbsp |
| 2 dashes | Hot Pepper Sauce | 2 dashes |
| ½ | Lime (juiced) | ½ |
| | Capers | |
| 5 slices | White Bread | 5 slices |

Have the marlin sliced thinly. With a sharp breadknife cut the crusts off the bread. Combine softened cream cheese, chives, hot pepper sauce and lime juice. Blend well. Spread the bread slices with cream cheese mixture. Cover the slices completely with the marlin, then cut each into four triangles. With a small star tip, pipe a star in the middle of each triangle and top with a caper. Arrange of a serving dish and garnish with parsley or watercress. Serves 6.

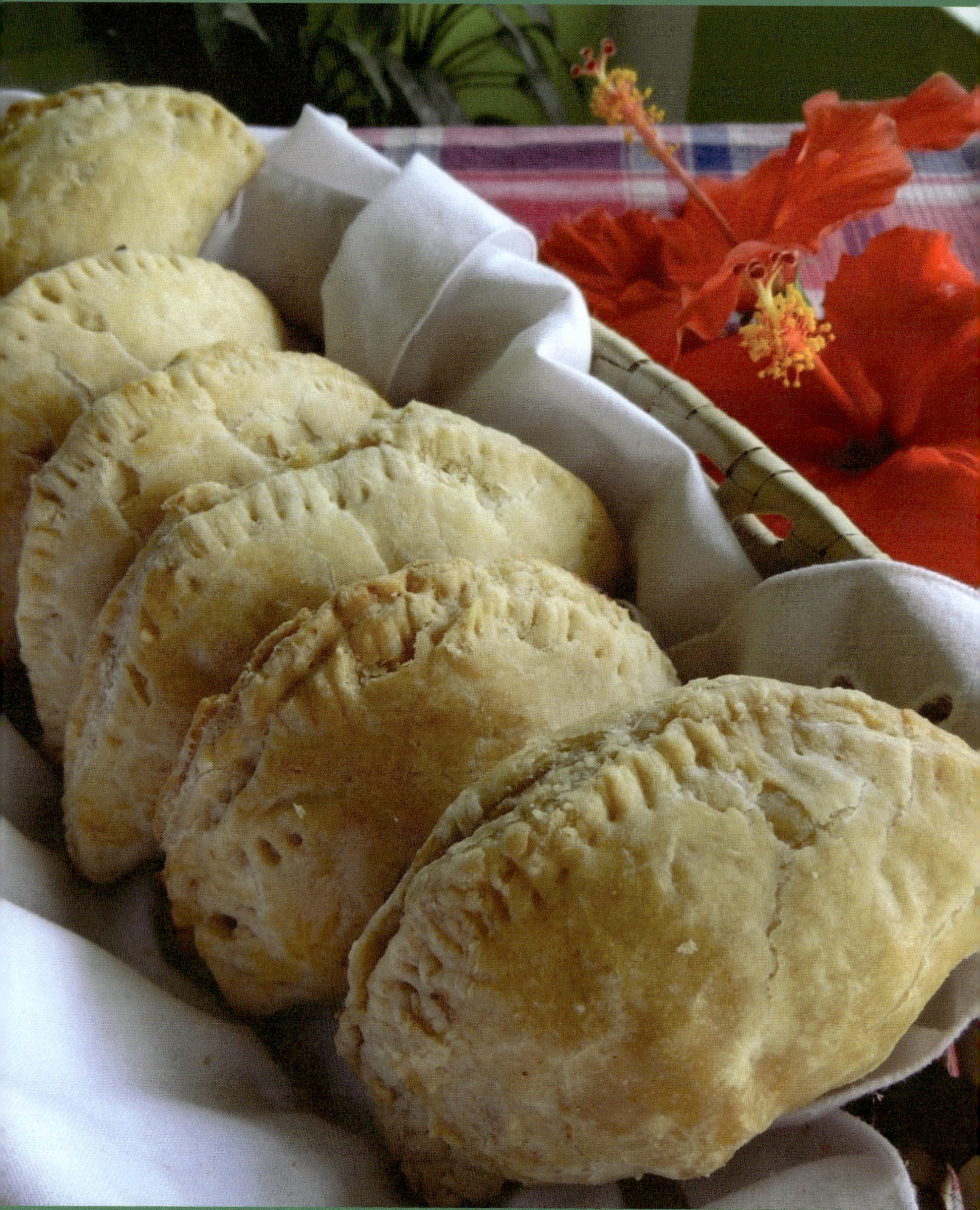

# BEEF PATTIES

A patty is one of the most typically Jamaican foods that you can enjoy. Patties come in different sizes-from full-sized lunch to small cocktail ones for teas, parties and meetings. The first patties were always beef, but now various fillings like vegetable, chicken, and shrimp are readily available.

| | | |
|---|---|---|
| 1 ½ lbs | Ground Beef | 650 g |
| 1 tsp. | Salt | 1 tsp. |
| 1 tbsp | Cooking Oil | 1 tbsp |
| 1 med | Onion | 1 med |
| 2 large cloves | Garlic | 2 large cloves |
| 2 stalks | Scallion | 2 stalks |
| 1 sm. | Scotch Bonnet Pepper | 1 sm |
| 1 large sprig | Fresh thyme | 1 large spig |
| | Or | |
| 1 tsp | Dried thyme | 1 tsp |
| ½ cup | Breadcrumbs | 60 g |
| | Patty Dough (p 14...) | |

Finely chop onion, scallion, garlic and fresh pepper, if used. In large skillet, heat cooking oil and add ground beef, salt, the chopped seasonings and thyme all at once. Cook, stirring often until the red in the meat disappears. Add breadcrumbs and about 2 cups/500 ml of water. Cover and simmer on low heat for about 20 minutes. Remove from heat and cool completely. Filling will thicken as it cools so it might seem runny when hot. On a floured surface, roll out patty dough with a large rolling pin. Cut into 6"/15 cm circles and place 3-4 tbsps of beef filling on each circle. Fold over and crimp edges securely. Place on a greased baking sheet and bake in a preheated 350 F oven for about 20 minutes. For cocktail-sized patties cut out 4"/10 cm circles and place 2 t bsps. of filling on each one. Fold, crimp and bake in preheated 325 F oven for 15 minutes. Serve hot. Makes 8 large or 20 cocktail patties.

APPETIZERS

# PATTY DOUGH

| | | |
|---|---|---|
| 2 lbs. | All-purpose flour | 1 kg. |
| ¼ cup | Sugar | 60 g |
| 2 tsp | Salt | 2 tsp. |
| 12 ozs. | Shortening | 350 g. |
| | Iced Water | |
| 5-6 drops | Yellow or Orange Food Colouring | |

Sift together flour, sugar and salt twice in large bowl. Cut in shortening until flour mixture resembles coarse breadcrumbs.

Add food colouring to the iced water and mix well. Pour over flour mixture and stir lightly to make a pliant dough. Roll out with a large rolling pin on a floured surface to make a rectangle. Starting at the narrow end, fold over a third onto itself then fold the other third over that so you end up with dough being 3 thick. Roll out to original size and fold again. Place in refrigerator for 3 to 4 hours. Roll to original size and fold again. Place once again in fridge for 3 to 4 hours. Roll out to original size and fold again. Roll out to 1/8 in and cut out circles to the desired size to make the patties.

## SHORTCRUST PASTRY

| | | |
|---|---|---|
| 3 cups | Flour | 340 g |
| 4 ozs | Butter or Shortening | 120 g |
| 1/2 tsp | Salt | 1/2 tsp |
| | Iced Water | |

Sift flour and salt together in a medium bowl. Prepare about 1 cup of iced water and set aside. Cut butter or shortening into flour mixture until it looks like coarse breadcrumbs. Bind with enough iced water to make a soft but not sticky dough. With a rolling pin, roll out on a floured surface to desired thickness and use as required for recipe.

# SOUPS

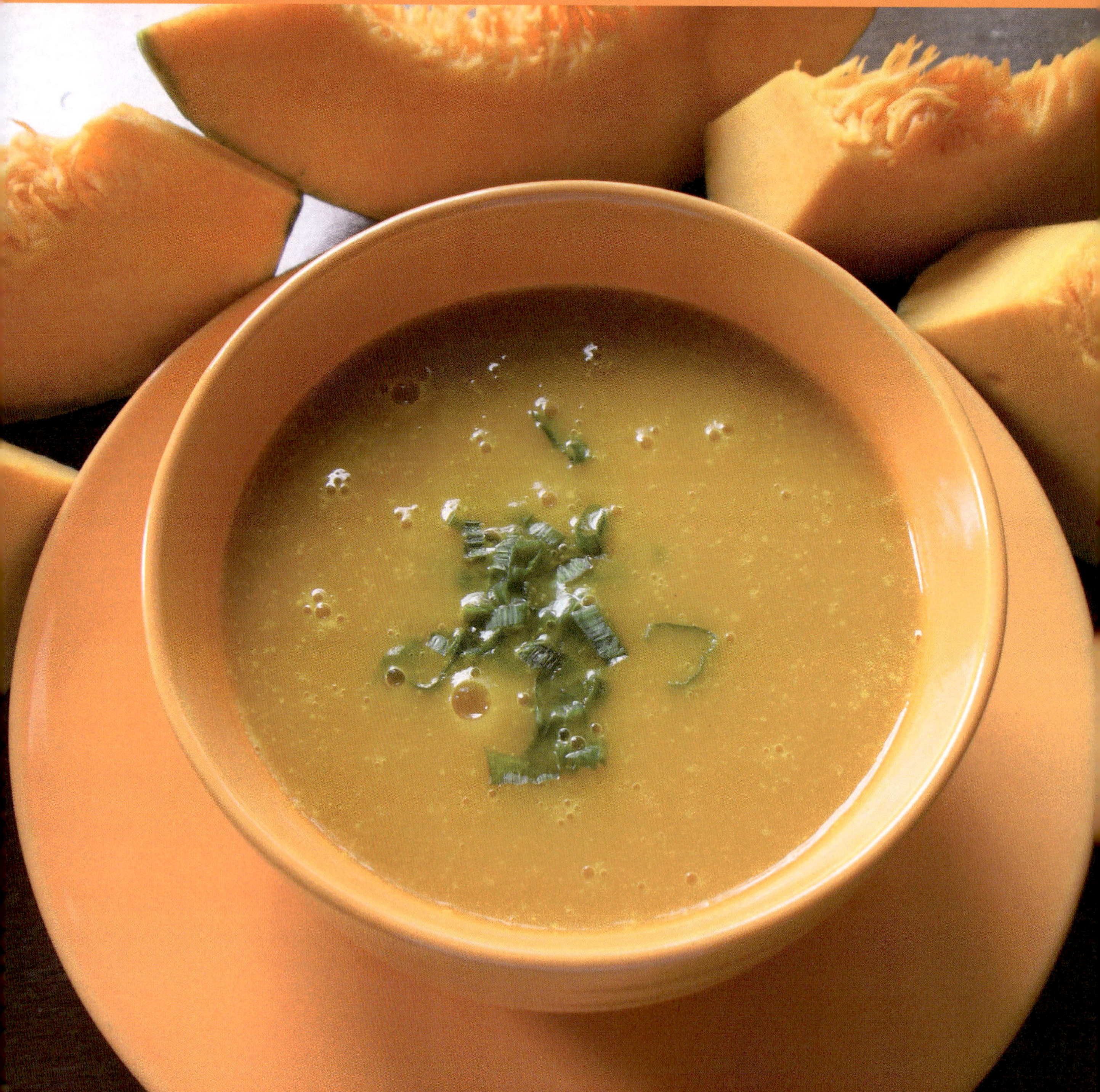

# PUMPKIN BEEF SOUP

The Calabaza variety of pumpkin is widely used in Jamaican cuisine. It has a dry dense texture and a bright orange colour. When a whole pumpkin is cut, inexplicably, beads of moisture appear on the cut surface. So, when Jamaicans say, "you a go find out how water walk go a pumpkin belly" they mean you're going to find out something that you'd rather not know.

| | | |
|---|---|---|
| 2 lb. | Pumpkin | 900 g. |
| 1 ½ lbs | Soupbeef | 700 g. |
| | Salt | |
| 1 tsp | Black Pepper | 1 tsp |
| 1 large | Onion | 1 large |
| 2 stalks | Scallion | 2 stalks |
| 1 tbsp | Thyme | 1 tbsp |
| | or | |
| 2 tsp. | Dried Thyme | 2 tsp. |
| 3 cloves | Garlic | 3 cloves |
| 1 | Scotch Bonnet pepper | 1 |
| | or | |
| 2 tsp. | Crushed Peppers | 2 tsp |
| 1 lb | Yam | 450 g |
| 1/2 lb | Dasheen or Coco | 225 g |

Peel pumpkin and cut into large cubes. Peel and chop onion coarsely. Peel and chop scallion and crush garlic. In 10-quart/10-liter pot, combine about 1 gallon/4 liters of water with the pumpkin, about a tablespoon of salt, black pepper, onion, scallion, thyme, garlic and Scotch Bonnet pepper and bring to a boil over high heat. Cut the meat into cubes and add to pot. Cover, lower heat to medium and simmer for about two hours, stirring occasionally. Expect the pumpkin to fall apart during this simmering. Peel yam and dasheen or coco, cut in large chunks and add to soup. When root vegetables are fork-tender, taste for salt and add accordingly.

If a soup of the pumpkin puree only is desired, as perhaps for a first course, the root vegetables can be omitted, the soup can be allowed to cool, the meat removed and the liquid then blended smooth in a blender. The soup can be then returned to the pot, reheated, tasted for salt and served. In all cases, the soup must be served piping hot. Serves between 10-16.

SOUPS

# CHICKEN SOUP

| | | |
|---|---|---|
| 2 lbs | Chicken | 900 grams |
| 1 ½ lbs | Pumpkin | 700 grams |
| 1 tbsp | Salt | 1 tbsp. |
| 2 large | Onions | 2 large |
| 3 stalks | Scallion | 3 stalks |
| 1 | Scotch Bonnet Pepper | 1 |
| 4 cloves | Garlic | 4 cloves |
| 1 tbsp | Thyme | 1 tbsp. |
| | or | |
| 2 tsp. | Dried Thyme | 2 tsp. |
| 1 lbs | Yam | 450 grams |
| 1/2 lb | Dasheen or Coco | 225 |
| 2 cups | Flour | 225 grams |

Rinse chicken under cold running water. Remove skin and cut in small pieces. Set aside. Peel pumpkin and cut in large chunks. Peel and chop onions coarsely. Mash and peel garlic. Peel and chop scallion. In 10-quart/10 liter pot, pour about 6 quarts/6 liters water and add pumpkin, salt, onions, scallion, pepper, garlic and thyme. Bring to a rolling boil. Add chicken. Return to boil and then lower heat to medium. Simmer for about 90 minutes, stirring occasionally. Peel root vegetables, cut into chunks and add to pot. In medium bowl place flour and add enough water to make a firm dough. Pull off 1-tablespoon pieces and shape into small dumplings and add to soup. Simmer for another 30 minutes and then taste for salt.

Serve piping hot. Makes about 14 servings.

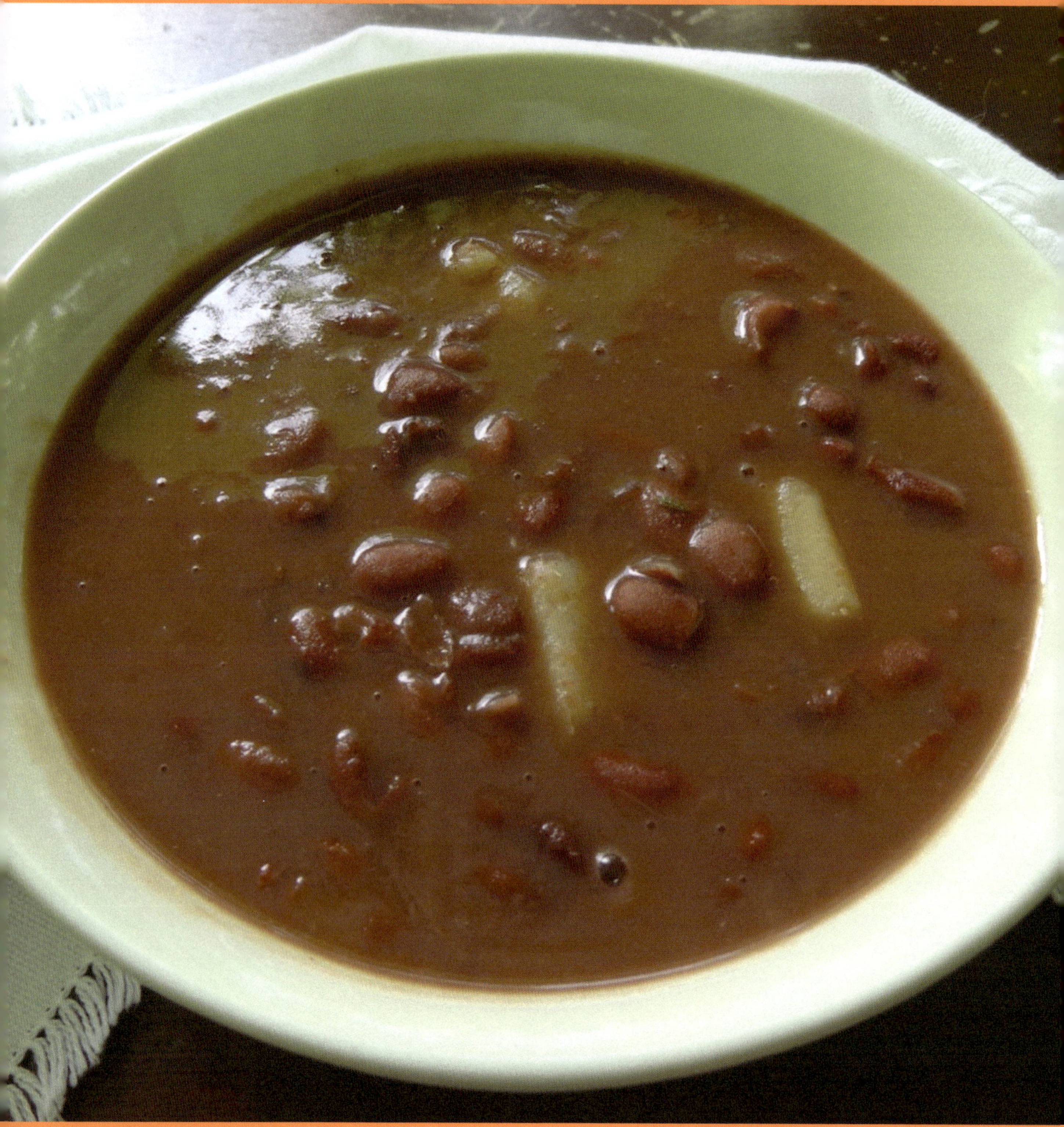

# RED PEAS SOUP

| | | |
|---|---|---|
| 12 ozs. | Red peas | 340 grams |
| 1 lb | Corned or Salted meat | 450 grams |
| ½ lb | Stewing beef | 225 grams |
| 2 large | Onions | 2 large |
| 3 stalks | Scallion | 3 stalks |
| 3 cloves | Garlic | 3 cloves |
| 1 | Scotch Bonnet Pepper | 1 |
| | or | |
| 2 tsp | Crushed Peppers | 2 tsp |
| 1 tbsp | Thyme | 1 tbsp |
| | or | |
| 2 tsp | Dried Thyme | 2 tsp |
| 1 lb | Root Vegetables (yam and coco) | 450 g |
| 2 cups | Flour | 225 g |

Wash salted meat thoroughly under cold running water. In large bowl, cover with water and soak overnight. Drain.

Peel and chop onions coarsely. Peel and chop scallion. Peel and mash garlic. Measure about 1 gallon /4 liters of water into a 10- quart/ 10-liter pot. Add the peas and all the meat and place over high heat. Add the onions, scallion, garlic, pepper and thyme. Allow to come to a vigourous boil. Lower heat and simmer for about 2 hours, stirring occasionally. Peel root vegetables, cut into chunks and add to pot. In medium bowl, place flour and add enough cold water to make a firm dough. Pull off 1-tablespoon pieces, shape into dumplings and add to pot. Simmer for another 30 minutes. Taste for salt. Serve piping hot.

Serves 12-14.

# PEPPERPOT SOUP

| | | |
|---|---|---|
| 1 lb | Callaloo | 450 grams |
| 2 large | Onions | 2 large |
| 2 stalks | Scallion | 2 stalks |
| 3 cloves | Garlic | 3 cloves |
| 1 | Scotch Bonnet Pepper | 1 |
| 2 tsp. | Thyme | 2 tsp |
| | or | |
| 1 tsp | Dried Thyme | 1 tsp |
| 2 tbsp | Oil | 2 tbsp |
| | Salt | |
| 1 lb. | Salted or Corned Meat | 450 grams |
| 12 ozs. | Coco | 340 grams |
| 12 ozs | White Yam | 340 g |

Wash the salted meat thoroughlly under cold running water. In a large bowl, cover with cold water and soak for at least 6 hours or overnight. Drain.

Select fresh, dark green callaloo with tender stems. Wash thoroughly under cold water, removing any blossoms. Slice thinly. Peel and chop onions. Peel and chop scallion. Mash and peel garlic cloves. In a large skillet, pour the oil. Add the callaloo, the onion, scallion, garlic, pepper, thyme and a sprinkling of salt. Cover the skillet and steam for about 15 minutes. Measure about 6 quarts/6 liters of water in a 10-quart/10-liter pot. Add the meat and the steamed callaloo. Bring to a boil. Lower the heat and simmer for about 90 minutes. Peel both the coco and white yam, cut into chunks and add to pot. Simmer for another 45 minutes stirring occasionally. Expect the soup to thicken a bit at this point as the coco will add texture. Test for salt. Serve piping hot.

Serves about 12-14.

If callaloo is not available, use the same weight of fresh spinach. Today, the coco and the different varieties of yam are available at Caribbean shops throughout North America and England.

# GUNGO PEAS SOUP

Fresh gungo peas are an integral part of the festive season in Jamaica. The cool month of December is harvest time for these pale green peas and they soon find themselves nestled in rice and peas or swimming in a soup or stew. Although the delicate flavour of the fresh gungo is savoured, part of the crop is always dried to be used in the New Year.

| | | |
|---|---|---|
| 3 cups | Fresh Gungo Peas | 750 ml |
| | or | |
| 1 ½ cups | Dried Gungo Peas | 375 ml |
| 1 lb | Salted Meat | 450 g |
| 2 large | Onions | 2 large |
| 3 cloves | Garlic | 3 cloves |
| 1 | Scotch Bonnet Pepper | 1 |
| 1 tbsp | Fresh Thyme | 1 tbsp |
| | or | |
| 2 tsp | Dried Thyme | 2 tsp |
| 1 ½ lbs | Assorted Yam | 700 grams |
| 1 cup | Flour | 125 g |

If dried peas are being used, wash and pick them, then soak overnight in cold water.

Wash salted meat under cold running water. In a large bowl, cover with water and soak for at least 6 hours or overnight. Drain.

Measure about 1 gallon/4 liters of water in a 10-quart/10-liter pot, add the peas, fresh or dried, and meat and set over high heat. While it is coming to a boil, peel and chop the onions and mash and peel the garlic. Add onions, garlic, pepper and thyme to pot and allow to come to a rolling boil. Lower heat and simmer for about 90 minutes. Peel yam, cut into chunks and add to pot. In a bowl, place flour and add enough cold water to make a stiff dough. Pull off 1-tablespoon pieces, shape into dumplings and add to soup. Simmer for a further 30-45 minutes, stirring occasionally. Remove the thyme sprig, if a sprig was used. Serve very hot.

Makes about 12-14 servings.

# FISH TEA

| | | |
|---|---|---|
| 2 lbs | Fish | 900 g |
| 1 lb | pumpkin | 450 g |
| | Salt | |
| 3 large | Onions | 3 large |
| 4 large cloves | Garlic | 4 large cloves |
| 1 whole | Scotch Bonnet Pepper | 1 whole |
| 1 tbsp | Thyme | 1 tbsp |
| | or | |
| 2 tsp | Dried Thyme | 2 tsp |
| 1 lb | Yam (white and yellow) | 450 g |
| ½ lb | Coco | 225 g |
| 3-4 | Okras | 3-4 |
| 4 ozs. | Shrimps (optional) | 125 g |

The traditional fish used for this recipe are maccaback and welshman which are small, bony fish ideal for soup. Amounts of snapper, goatfish and butterfish could also be added to the smaller fish to make up the weight. In the absence of the maccaback and welshman the larger fish only can be used.

Have whatever fish you use scaled and cleaned but maintain the heads. Peel the pumpkin and cut into chunks. Peel and chop onions coarsely. Peel and crush garlic. Add 1 gallon/4 liters of water to a 10qt/10 liter pot. Add the fish, pumpkin, salt, onions, garlic, pepper and thyme. Bring to a boil. Lower heat and simmer for about and hour, stirring occasionally. Peel yam and coco and cut into chunks. Add to pot. Remove stems from okras and slice. Add to fish tea. Simmer for a further 20 minutes. Taste for salt. Remove thyme sprig, if used.

If desired, add the shrimp, whole or headless, shelled or unshelled, to the simmering soup after the okras.

Serve piping hot. Serves about 14.

# MANNISH WATER

| | | |
|---|---|---|
| 2 lbs. | Goat head and belly | 900 g |
| 2 large | Onions | 2 large |
| 4 cloves | Garlic | 4 cloves |
| 1 | Scotch Bonnet Pepper | 1 |
| 1 tsp. | Thyme (fresh) | 1 tsp |
| | Or | |
| ½ tsp | Dried Thyme | ½ tsp |
| 1 | Carrot | 1 |
| | Salt | |
| 4 | Green Bananas | 4 |
| ½ lb. ea. | Yam, Coco and Dasheen | 225 g |

The goat head and belly should be cut in small pieces by the butcher. Clean and wash in cold running water. Peel and slice onions, peel and crush garlic. Scrape carrot and cut in small pieces. Bring about 6 quarts/6 liters of water and a tablespoon of salt to boil over high heat in a 10-quart pot. Add the goat head and belly, the onions, garlic, pepper, thyme. Return to a rolling boil, then reduce heat to low. Simmer for about 2 hours. Peel bananas, dasheen, yam and coco and cut into medium chunks. Add along with carrot to pot. Continue simmering until meat is tender. While simmering, taste for salt and add accordingly. Serve hot.

About 15 servings

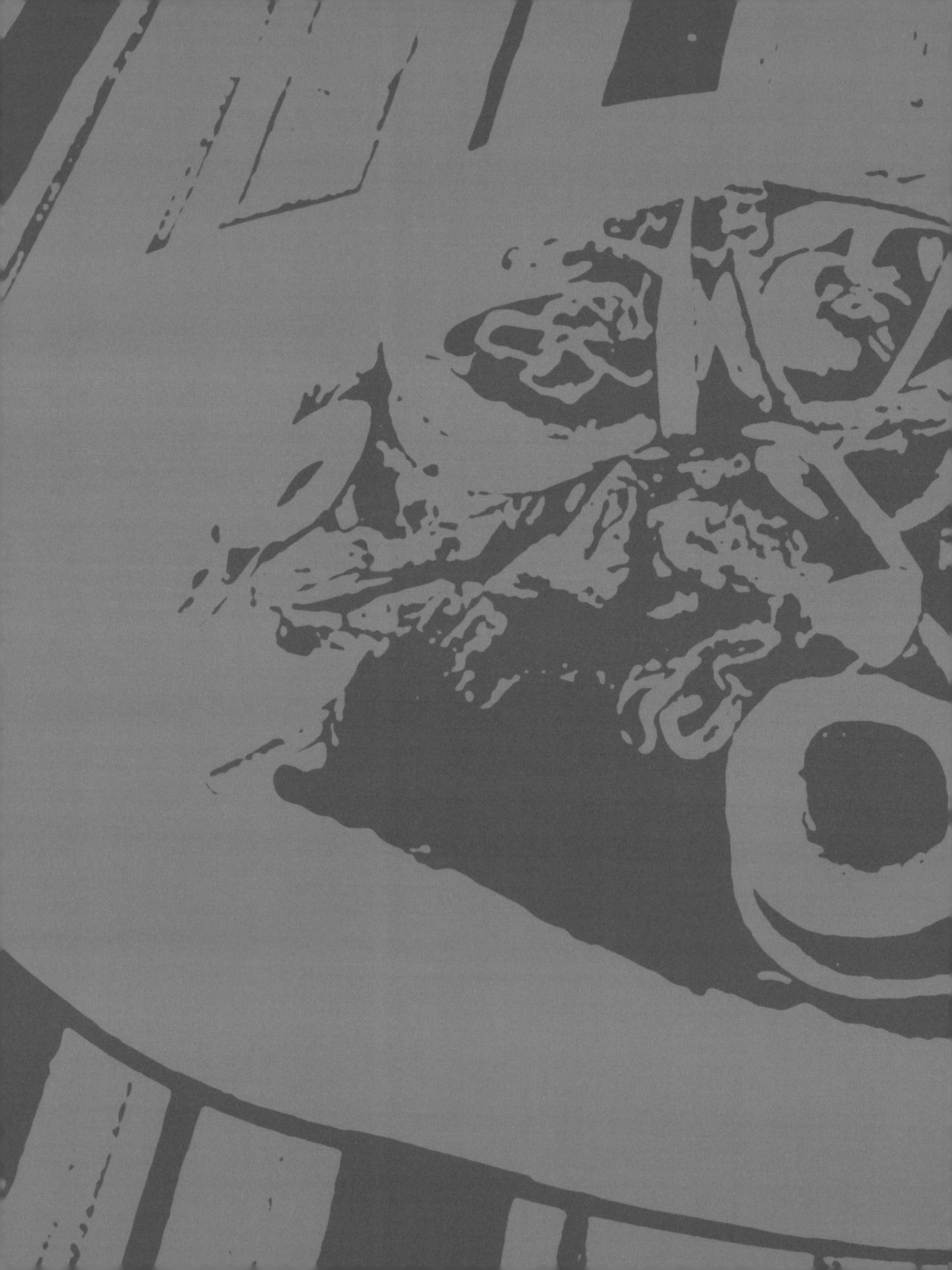

# MAIN DISHES

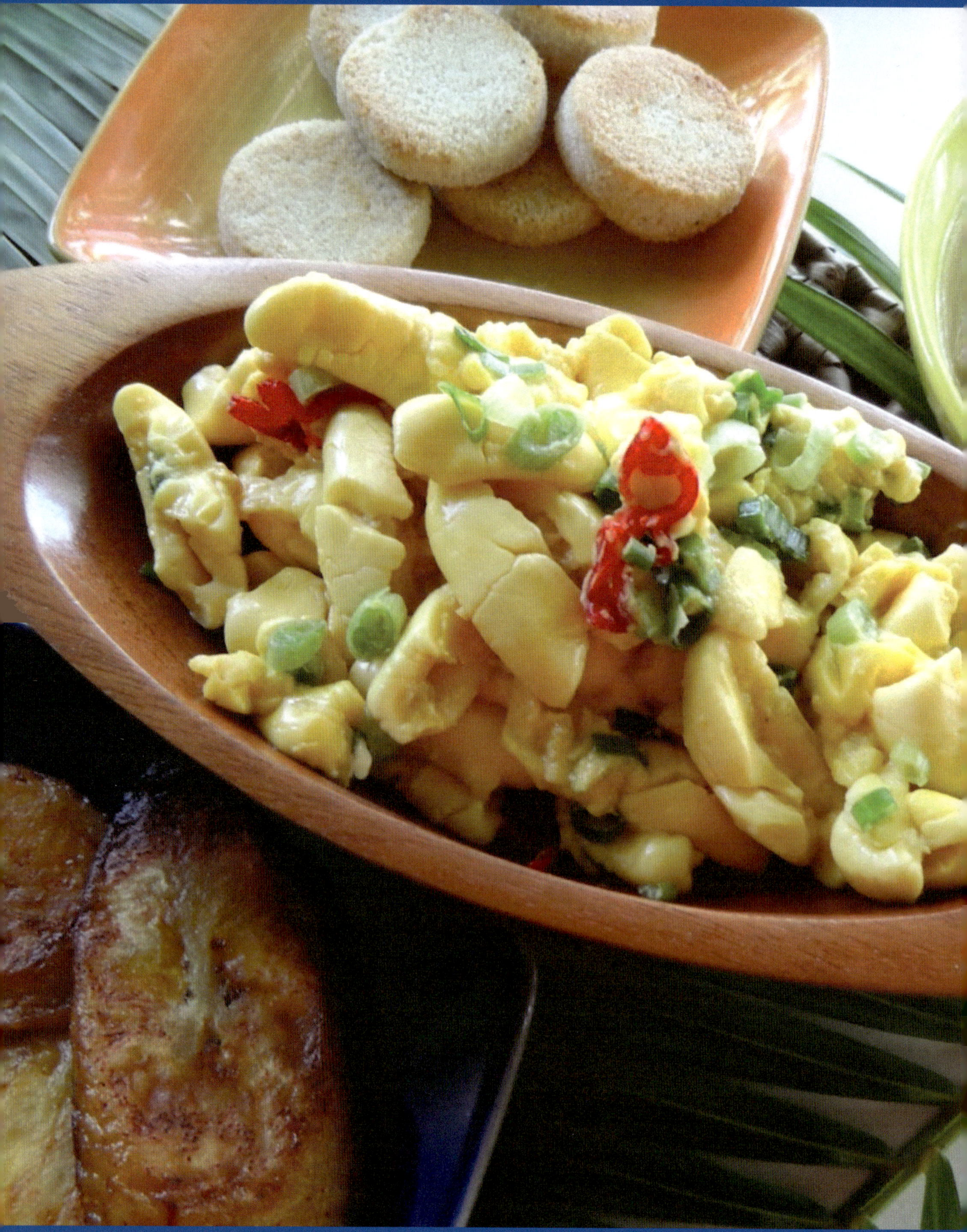

# ACKEE AND SALTFISH

This dish is our national dish, beloved by Jamaicans everywhere. That ackee and saltfish became elevated to this status bears striking irony, in that the ackee tree is an import from West Africa that grows very well in the Caribbean and saltfish is a product of the Canadian or Norwegian fishing industry. In the other Caribbean islands, the the trees grow but the fruit is not eaten, causing Jamaicans to always shake their heads and lament, "What a waste!"

| | | |
|---|---|---|
| 12 | Ackee Pods | 12 |
| 2 tsp | Salt | 2 tsp |
| 3 ozs. | Salted Codfish | 60 grams |
| 4 tbsp | Oil | 4 tbsp |
| 1 | Medium Onion | 1 |
| 3 stalks | Scallion | 3 stalks |
| 2 cloves | Garlic | 2 cloves |
| 1 tsp | Scotch Bonnet Pepper | 1tsp |
| | or | |
| 1tsp | Crushed Pepper | 1 tsp |
| 1 tsp | Fresh Thyme | 1 tsp |
| | or | |
| ½ tsp | Dried Thyme | ½ tsp |
| ½ tsp | Black Pepper | ½ tsp |

Wash and soak fish in water for about 2 hours.

Remove yellow fruit from ackee pods. Remove black seeds and pink membranes from fruit. Rinse under cold running water. **Never leave raw ackee soaking in water.** Half-fill a medium saucepan with water, add salt and bring to boil. Add ackee and cook until ackee is fork-tender, about 15 minutes. When cooked, drain and set aside.

While ackee is cooking, remove skin, scales, bones and fins from fish, flake and set aside. Slice onion and scallion thinly and if using fresh pepper, dice finely. Peel and mince garlic. In medium frying pan heat oil over high heat. Add onion, scallion, fresh Scotch Bonnet or crushed pepper and garlic and sauté till slightly browned. Add fish and thyme and cook for a further five minutes, stirring occasionally. Add drained ackee and black pepper and combine well. Cook for about 8- 10 minutes. Serve hot with bammy, boiled bananas or fried dumplings. Serves 4.

Note- A 20-oz. can of ackee, drained, can be used instead of fresh.

MAIN DISHES

# ESCOVEITCHED FISH

| | | |
|---|---|---|
| 3 lbs | Fresh Fish | 1 ½ kg |
| 4 tsp | Salt | 4 tsp |
| 4 tsp | Black Pepper | 4 tsp |
| 1 | Scotch Bonnet Pepper | 1 |
| | or | |
| 1 tbsp | Bottled Crushed Pepper | 1 tbsp |
| 1 cup | Oil | 250 ml |
| 2 cups | White or Malt Vinegar | 500 ml |
| 1 tbsp | Whole Pimento Seeds | 1 tbsp |
| 2 large | Onions | 2 large |
| 1 med | Carrots | 1 med |

Use kingfish, snapper, jack, goatfish or sprats. If using a large fish, slice in ¾ "/2 cm slices. If smaller fish are used, leave whole. Have the fish-seller gut and scale fish.

Combine the salt and black pepper and sprinkle the entire surface of the fish inside and out with this. In a large frying pan, heat oil until there are small ripples on the surface. Place fish in frying pan, fry on both sides till golden–brown. As fish is done, remove from oil and drain on absorbent paper. Set aside in a deep dish.

Peel and thinly slice onions. Slice carrot either in julienne strips or in thin circles. If using fresh Scotch Bonnet, slice in thin strips. In small saucepan combine vinegar, fresh or crushed pepper, pimento seeds, onions and carrots over high heat and bring to boil. Lower heat to medium and simmer for about 5 minutes or until vegetables are just tender-crisp. Remove from heat and pour over fish. Serve either hot or room temperature.

Serves 6 –8

# SALT FISH AND GARDEN EGG (EGG PLANT)

| | | |
|---|---|---|
| 1 lb | Salted Codfish | 450g |
| 1 large | Garden Egg(Eggplant) | 1 large |
| 1 large | Onion | 1 large |
| 3 cloves | Garlic | 3 cloves |
| 2 stalks | Scallion | 2 stalks |
| large sprig | Thyme(fresh) | large Sprig |
| | Or | |
| 1½ tsp. | Thyme (dried) | 1½ tsp. |
| 1 tsp. | Scotch Bonnet Pepper(slivered) | 1 tsp. |
| | Or | |
| 1 tsp. | Hot Pepper Sauce | 1 tsp. |
| 4 | Plum Tomatoes (ripe) | 4 |
| ¼ cup | Coconut Oil | 60 ml |

Wash off the large grains of salt that might be clinging to fish and place in small bowl and just cover with water. Soak for 4-6 hours. Remove from water and with a sharp knife, remove all skin, scales, fins and bones. Flake fish and set aside.

Wash garden egg and remove the stem end. Cut into ¼" slices. Peel and slice onion and scallion. Dice tomatoes. Peel and crush garlic.

Use a large, heavy skillet with a cover. Heat oil until ripples form and add onion, scallion, garlic, pepper and thyme. Sauté lightly as you keep the vegetables moving. Add fish and tomato and continue to sauté and combine well. Place garden egg slices in a layer over fish and cover skillet. Turn heat to low and cook for about 20 minutes. Stir gently to combine during the cooking time.

Serve hot with boiled rice and boiled green bananas.

6 servings.

MAIN DISHES

# MACKEREL RUNDOWN

The ideal accompaniment for this dish is boiled green bananas as well as boiled dumplings or any kind of yam.

| | | |
|---|---|---|
| 1 ½ lbs | Salted Mackerel | 675 gr. |
| 1 large | Coconut | 1 large |
| 1 tsp | Scotch Bonnet Pepper or | 1 tsp. |
| 2 tsp | Crushed Pepper | 2 tsp. |
| 2 cloves | Garlic | 2 cloves |
| 2 small | Tomatoes | 2 small |
| 1 large | Onion | 1 large |
| 3 stalks | Scallion | 3 stalks |
| ½ tsp | Fresh Thyme or | ½ tsp |
| ¼ tsp | Dried Thyme | ¼ tsp |

Wash mackerel under cold running water, to remove the large grains of salt. In large bowl, cover with at least 2 quarts /2 liters cold water and soak for at least 6 hours, changing the water once. Drain. Then remove fins, skin and bones. Set aside.

Crack coconut open, saving the water. With a small, sharp knife remove the white flesh from the shell. Grate the flesh and combine with about 3 cups/750 ml of water mixing well. Strain off the juice using a large sieve, pressing down with the back of a large spoon on the coconut to extract all. Pour juice into medium sized frying pan with a cover and place over high heat. Peel and crush the garlic cloves and peel and slice onion. Dice tomatoes and peel and slice scallions, including the green tops. Add garlic, onion, tomato, scallion, thyme, and fresh Scotch Bonnet or crushed pepper to coconut juice and bring to a boil. Lower heat and simmer gently for about 20 minutes until the "custard" forms and rises to the top of the liquid. Add mackerel and simmer for about 15-20 minutes more. Serve hot.

Note-A 13-oz can of unsweetened coconut cream can be substituted for the fresh coconut. Add enough water to make 3 cups.

# FRICASSE CHICKEN

Most Jamaicans don't consider Sundays complete without this savoury chicken stew for family dinner with all the trimmings.

| | | |
|---|---|---|
| 13-lb | Chicken | 1½ kg |
| | Salt | |
| | Black Pepper | |
| 1 tbsp | Dark Soy Sauce | 1 tbsp. |
| 2 med | Onions | 2 med |
| 3 cloves | Garlic | 3 cloves |
| 3 stalks | Scallion | 3 stalks |
| 1 | Scotch Bonnet Pepper | 1 |
| | or | |
| 2 tsp. | Crushed Peppers | 2 tsp. |
| 3 tbsp | Oil | 3 tbsp. |
| 1 tsp | Fresh Thyme | 1 tsp. |
| | or | |
| ½ tsp | Dried Thyme | ½ tsp |
| 2 med | Ripe Tomatoes | 2 med |
| 1 sm | Sweet Pepper | 1 sm (if desired) |
| 1 tbsp | Flour | 1 tbsp |

Wash chicken under cold running water inside and out. Joint the chicken. Don't wash again.

Dice onions and garlic finely. Slice scallion thinly. If using fresh pepper, remove seeds and slice thinly. Dice tomatoes and sweet pepper, if used. In a large enough bowl to move the chicken around freely, season with soy sauce, salt, black pepper, onions, garlic, scallion, thyme and fresh or crushed pepper. Combine well making sure all surfaces of the chicken are covered with the seasonings.

Using a heavy Dutch pot, heat oil over a high flame until it ripples. Drop chicken in pot piece by piece, and brown on both sides. After all the chicken is browned, drop vegetables in pot and brown slightly, making sure no burning takes place. Add 1 cup/250 ml of water to pot, cover, and lower heat to medium-low. Simmer for about 15 minutes. Add tomatoes and sweet pepper, if used. Add about another cup/250 ml of water and continue simmering for another 20 minutes. Dissolve the flour in a small amount of water and add to the pot stirring to thicken the gravy.

Serve hot. Serves 6.

# JERKED PORK

| | | |
|---|---|---|
| 2 lbs | Pork | 1 kg |
| | Salt | |
| 2 oz | Gingerroot | 60 g |
| 3 tbsp | Dark Soy Sauce | 3 tbsp. |
| 1 large | Scotch Bonnet Pepper | 1 large |
| 5 cloves | Garlic | 5 cloves |
| 5 stalks | Scallion | 5 stalks |
| 1 tbsp | Thyme (fresh) | 1 tbsp |
| | Or | |
| 2 tsps | Thyme (dried) | 2 tsps |
| 3 tbsp | Ground Pimento Seeds | 3 tbsp |

Use cuts of meat that have bone, skin and fat. Have the butcher cut the meat at 1 ½" intervals almost down to the bone.

Wash, peel and grate ginger and juice with about ½ cup/120 ml of water. Strain. Peel garlic and chop. Strip scallion and chop, making sure to use the green tops. Chop fresh pepper. Combine ginger juice, soy, pepper, garlic, scallion, thyme and ground pimento in a blender. Whirl for about 5 seconds.

Sprinkle the pork with salt. Rub the seasoning mixture into the meat with the back of a large spoon. At this point, pork can be left to marinate as long as overnight. Preheat oven to 350 F. Place pork in roasting pan with about 1 cup/250 ml of water in the bottom of the pan and roast pork for about 90 minutes, turning 2 or 3 times and making sure that the liquid doesn't dry out completely.

Serve hot. Serves 6.

Note- 1 tbsp. bottled crushed pepper can be substituted for fresh.

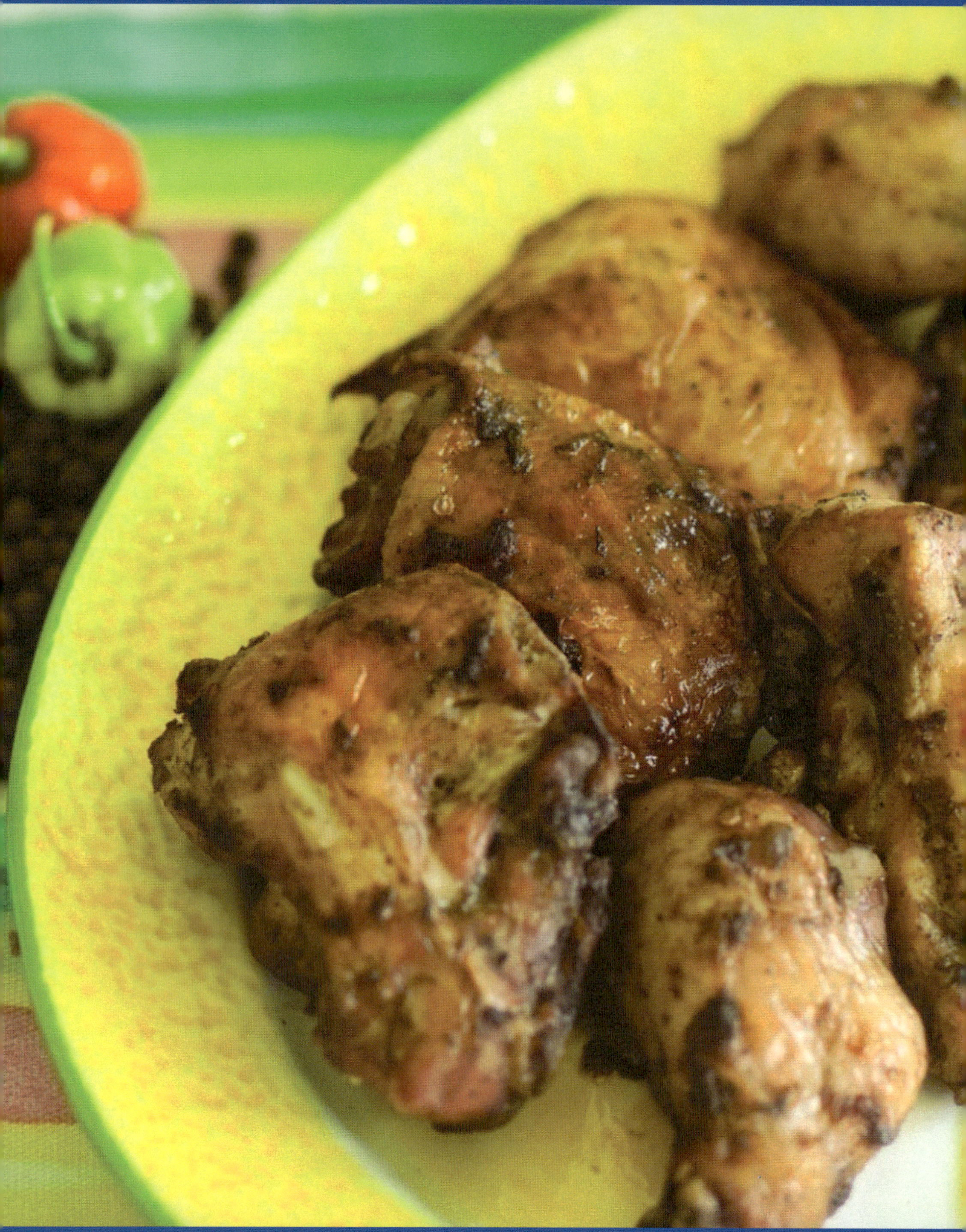

# JERKED CHICKEN

| | | |
|---|---|---|
| 3 lbs | Chicken | 1 ½ kg |
| | Salt | |
| 2 oz. | Fresh Gingerroot | 60 g. |
| 3 tbsp | Dark Soy Sauce | 3 tbsp. |
| 1 large | Scotch Bonnet Pepper | 1 large |
| 4 cloves | Garlic | 4 cloves |
| 4 stalks | Scallion | 4 stalks |
| 1 tbsp. | Fresh Thyme | 1 tbsp. |
| | or | |
| 2 tsps. | Dried Thyme | 2 tsps. |
| 3 tbsp | Ground Pimento Seeds | 3 tbsp. |

Use either desired chicken parts, or joint a whole bird. If using a whole bird, rinse inside and out with cold running water before jointing. **Do not rinse again after cutting.**

Preheat oven to 350 F.

Wash, peel and grate ginger. Juice with about ½ cup/120 ml. of water and strain. Peel garlic and chop. Strip scallion and slice, making sure to use the green tops. Finely chop fresh pepper, keeping the seeds, if used. Combine soy sauce, ginger juice, pepper, garlic, scallion, thyme and pimento in a blender. Whirl for about 5 seconds. Place chicken in a large bowl and sprinkle with salt. Add pimento mixture to chicken pieces and mix all round, making sure that all surfaces of the chicken are covered. In a large baking dish, lay chicken in a single layer, and add about 1 cup/250 ml of water to the bottom of the dish. Bake for 1 hour, turning pieces so that all sides are browned and making sure that the liquid doesn't dry out completely. Serves 5 or 6.

Note- 1 tbsp. bottled crushed pepper can be substituted for fresh.

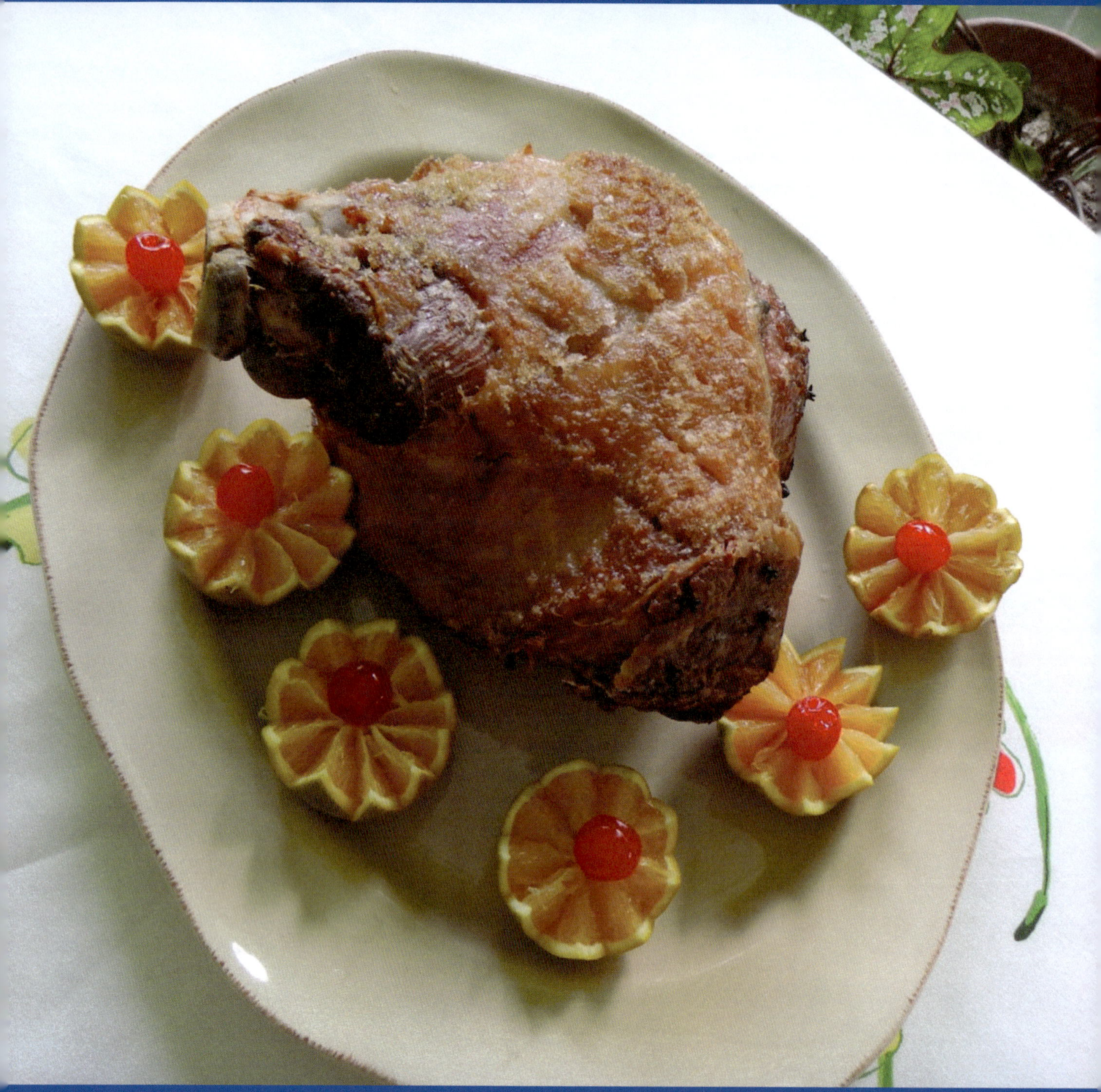

# ROASTED HAM

Ham

Cloves

Black Pepper

Brown Sugar

Choose desired cut of ham-shoulder or leg. Check tag for the exact weight. Remove all the plastic and muslin wrapping and rinse thoroughly under cold running water.

Preheat oven to 350°F. Place ham in baking dish of the appropriate size and add about 2 cups/500 ml of water. Stud with cloves, sprinkle with black pepper and place pan in oven. For every pound allow 15 minutes of ba ime. (For every kilogram, allow 30 minutes.) When there is about 30 minutes of baking time left, take baking pan out of oven and remove skin with a sharp knife, place in its own small baking pan and return to oven. Score the fat with the knife. Filling a large spoon with brown sugar, place on the exposed fat and rub in with the back of the spoon. The sugar will adhere very well. Return to oven for the remaining 30 minutes. The skin will make crackling during this time so check to make sure it does not burn. Remove ham at the end of the baking time and allow to rest for about 20 minutes before carving. On average, each pound of ham will serve four, each kilogram eight.

### MANGO-GINGER SAUCE

| 112-oz jar | Mango Jam | 1 375-ml jar |
| 2 ozs | Fresh Ginger | 60 g |

Wash and peel ginger. Either grate and combine with 4 ozs water or blend on high speed with 4 ozs water. Juice by pressing through strainer. Combine thoroughly with jam. Serve at room temperature with ham. Makes about 2 cups/500 ml.

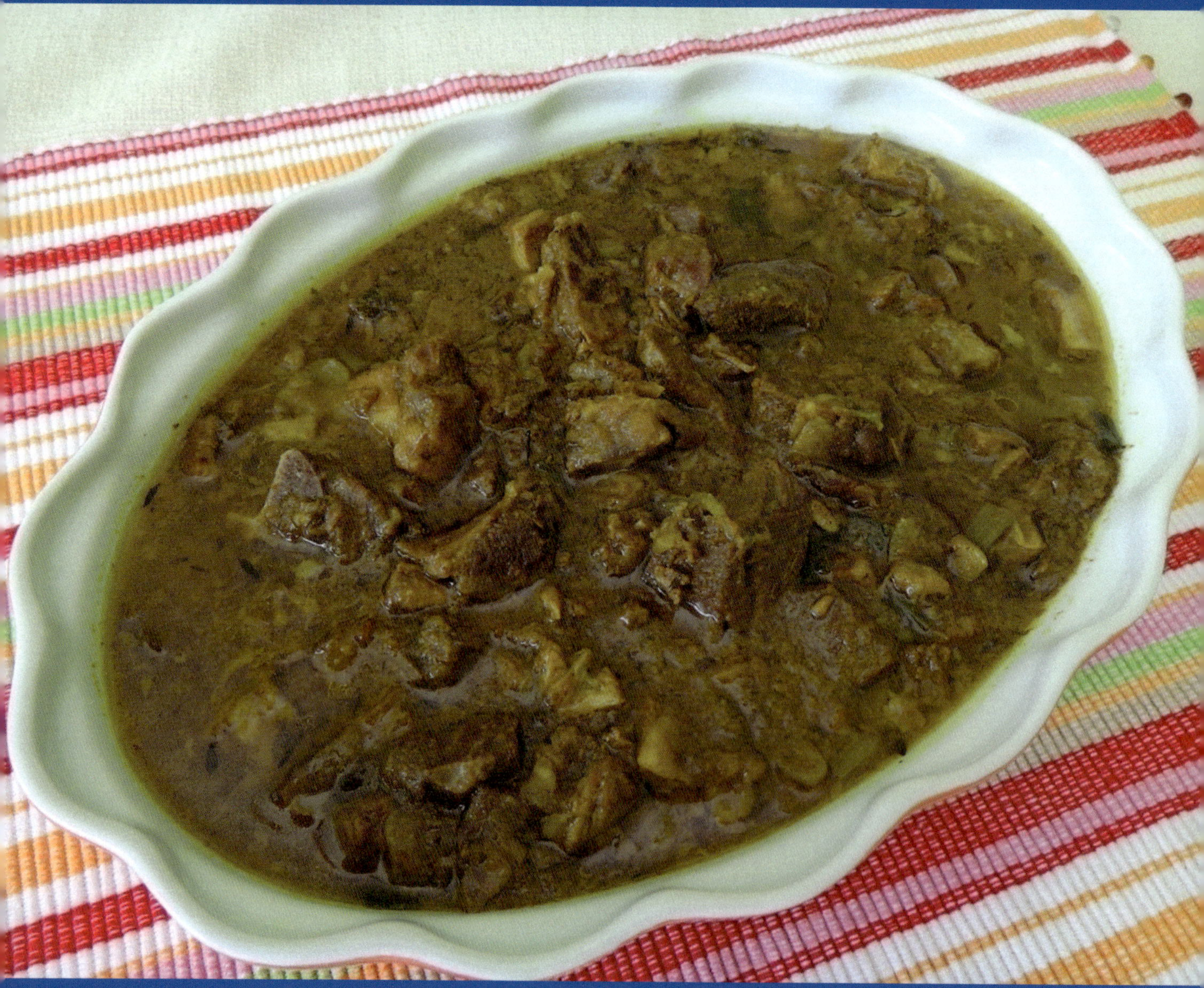

# CURRIED GOAT

| | | |
|---|---|---|
| 2 lbs. | Goat Meat | 1 kg. |
| | Salt | |
| | Black Pepper | |
| 1 | Onion (large) | 1 |
| 3 | Scallion stalks | 3 |
| 4 | Garlic Cloves | 4 |
| 1 | Scotch Bonnet Pepper | 1 |
| 2 tbsps | Thyme (fresh) | 2 tbsps. |
| | Or | |
| 1 tsp. | Thyme (dried) | 1 tsp. |
| 2 tbsp. | Curry Powder | 2 tbsp. |
| 3 tbsp. | Cooking Oil | 3 tbsp. |
| 1 | Large Irish Potato | 1 |
| | Boiling water | |

Goat meat is usually sold already cut in small pieces. If not, have the butcher do this.

Peel and chop onion coarsely, peel and crush garlic, peel and chop scallion, including the green tops and slice the pepper thinly, making sure not to touch it with your fingertips. In a large bowl, sprinkle goat with salt and black pepper. Add onion, scallion, garlic, Scotch Bonnet, thyme and mix very well, making sure that the seasonings are rubbed into all sides of the meat. In a medium-sized pot, heat the oil, and stir in the curry powder and allow to bubble for several seconds. Add the meat all at once, turning very well so that all pieces are coated with curry. Add about 2 cups/500 ml. boiling water and cover tightly. Turn heat down to low and simmer gently for about two hours, stirring occasionally and adding more boiling water, as needed.

When meat is almost tender, peel and dice potato and add to pot. Continue cooking until meat is tender.

Serve hot with rice and pineapple chutney.

Serves 6.

Lamb or mutton can be used interchangeably with goat.

MAIN DISHES

# CURRIED SHRIMPS

| | | |
|---|---|---|
| 1 lb. | Shrimp (headless) | 500 mg. |
| 1 | Onion(med.) | 1 |
| 3 | Garlic Cloves | 3 |
| 2 | Scallion Stalks | 2 |
| ½ | Scotch Bonnet Pepper | ½ |
| | Salt | |
| 1 tsp. | Thyme(fresh) | 1 tsp. |
| | Or | |
| ½ tsp. | Thyme(dried) | ½ tsp. |
| 2 tbsp. | Cooking Oil | 2 tbsp. |
| 1 tbsp. | Curry Powder | 1 tbsp. |
| 1 tsp. | Cornstarch | 1 tsp. |

**OPTIONAL:**

| | | |
|---|---|---|
| ¼ cup | Raisins | ¼ cup |

Use whatever size shrimps desired, from small to jumbo. Wash thoroughly under cold running water. Shell and devein. **Do not wash after this step.** Set aside.

Slice onion thinly, peel and mince garlic, peel and slice scallion including green tops and thinly slice pepper, making sure not to use your fingertips. Sprinkle shrimp with salt.

In heavy skillet, heat oil and stir in curry powder until oil bubbles. Add onion, scallion, garlic Scotch Bonnet and thyme and stir for several minutes as they cook. Add shrimp and cook for about 5 minutes more. If desired, add raisins at this point. Dissolve cornstarch in a small amount of water and add to skillet stirring until the gravy thickens.

Serve hot with rice.

4-5 servings.

# LOBSTERTAILS IN BUTTER SAUCE

The crustacean found in the Caribbean and commonly referred to as lobster in in fact a crayfish or spiny lobster and not the lobster found in Northern waters. It does not have large front claws, has very long, tapering antennae and the meat is a bit heavier and coarser than the Northern lobster, but every bit as delicious.

| | | |
|---|---|---|
| 2 | Lobstertails | 2 |
| 4 tbsp | Butter | 4 tbsp |
| 2 cloves | Garlic (minced) | 2 cloves |
| 1 | Onion(finely diced) | 1 |
| | White Pepper | |
| 2 | Limes | 2 |

Using a sharp knife, halve the tails, whether fresh or frozen. If using frozen, make sure to thaw thoroughly. Remove the intestinal vein.

Place a skillet on medium heat, and melt the butter. Add onion and garlic, 2 dashes of white pepper and the juice of one lime. Place the lobster halves, shell-side up, in the skillet, cover and allow to cook gently for about 15 minutes. Cut the second lime into wedges. Place tails on a platter, pour butter sauce over and decorate with lime wedges. Serve immediately.

# OXTAIL

| | | |
|---|---|---|
| 2 lbs. | Oxtail | 1 kg. |
| | Salt | |
| | Black Pepper | |
| 1 tbsp. | Soy sauce | 1 tbsp. |
| 1 | Onion (large) | 1 |
| 4 | Garlic Cloves | 4 |
| 1 | Scotch Bonnet Pepper | 1 |
| 2 tsp. | Thyme (fresh) | 2 tsp. |
| | Or | |
| 1 tsp. | Thyme (dried) | 1 tsp. |
| | Bay Leaf | |
| 3 | Plum Tomatoes (diced) | 3 |
| 1 sm. Can | Broad Beans | 1 sm can |

Sprinkle oxtail, that should be jointed, with salt, black pepper and soy sauce. Chop onions coarsely, crush garlic and thinly slice pepper, without touching with fingertips. Throw over oxtail. Heat oil in a heavy Dutch pot. Brown oxtail on all sides then add onions, garlic and Scotch Bonnet and cook slightly. Add about a quart/liter of **boiling** water to pot, along with the thyme and bay leaf. Cover tightly and simmer on low heat for about two hours. Add tomatoes. About 30 minutes later add broad beans and cook another 30 minutes. Add more boiling water as needed, stirring occasionally until meat is fork-tender. Remove bay leaf.

Serve hot with Rice and Peas. Serves 6.

# ROAST BEEF

| | | |
|---|---|---|
| 3-5 lbs | Beef | 1 ½ kg-2 ½ kg |
| | Salt | |
| | Black Pepper | |
| 5-7 cloves | Garlic | 5-7 cloves |
| 1 tbsp. | Thyme leaves | 1 tbsp. |
| 3-5 stalks | Scallion | 3-5 stalks |
| 2 tbsp. | Oil | 2 tbsp. |
| 1 | Onion (finely diced) | 1 |
| 1 tbsp. | Flour | 1 tbsp. |

Choose a cut to your liking, such as rib, round or sirloin roast.

A layer of fat will help to tenderize and flavour the meat.

Preheat oven to 375 F.

In a blender, combine the oil, garlic cloves, scallion and thyme leaves. Blend for about a minute. Sprinkle meat with salt and black pepper. Pour blended mixture over the meat and rub in well with the back of a spoon. Place a small roasting pan and add about ½ cup/125 ml of water to the bottom of pan. Roast for about 25 minutes per pound. Remove pan from oven and place roast on a platter. Place roaster over high heat and add the onion and about 1 cup of water in which the flour has been dissolved. Stir to deglaze pan and make the gravy. Allow roast to rest for about 20 minutes before carving. Serve with gravy. Allow between ¼ and 1/3 lb. uncooked meat per person. Otaheiti Apple Chutney goes well with this.

## STEWED PEAS

| | | |
|---|---|---|
| 12 ozs. | Red (kidney) beans | 325 g. |
| 1 lb. | Beef | 450 g |
| ½ lb. | Salted Meat | 225 g. |
| 1 | Onion (large) | 1 |
| 4 | Garlic cloves | 4 |
| 1 | Scotch Bonnet Pepper | 1 |
| 1 tsp. | Thyme (fresh) | 1 tsp. |
| | OR | |
| ½ tsp. | thyme (dried) | ½ tsp. |
| ½ cup | Diced Tomatoes | 125 ml. |
| 1 cup | Flour | 125 g. |

Use either salted pig's tail, corned pork or corned beef, depending on your taste. Rinse whatever meat used in cold running water, cover with water and soak overnight. In the morning discard water.

Wash beans and pick out any foreign material. Place beans and salted meat in a large pot and cover with cold water. Place on high heat and bring to a boil. While this is happening, cut fresh meat into cubes, peel and coarsely chop onion, peel and crush garlic. Add fresh beef, onion, garlic, pepper and thyme to pot. When liquid boils again, lower heat to low, cover tightly and simmer for about 1 hour, adding water if necessary. Add tomatoes to pot and simmer another 30 minutes.

In small bowl combine flour and a small amount of cold water to make a soft dough. Pull off small pieces and rub between palms to make long thin "spinners" and add to pot. Simmer until "spinners" are cooked, about another 15 minutes. Serve hot with white rice. Serves 6.

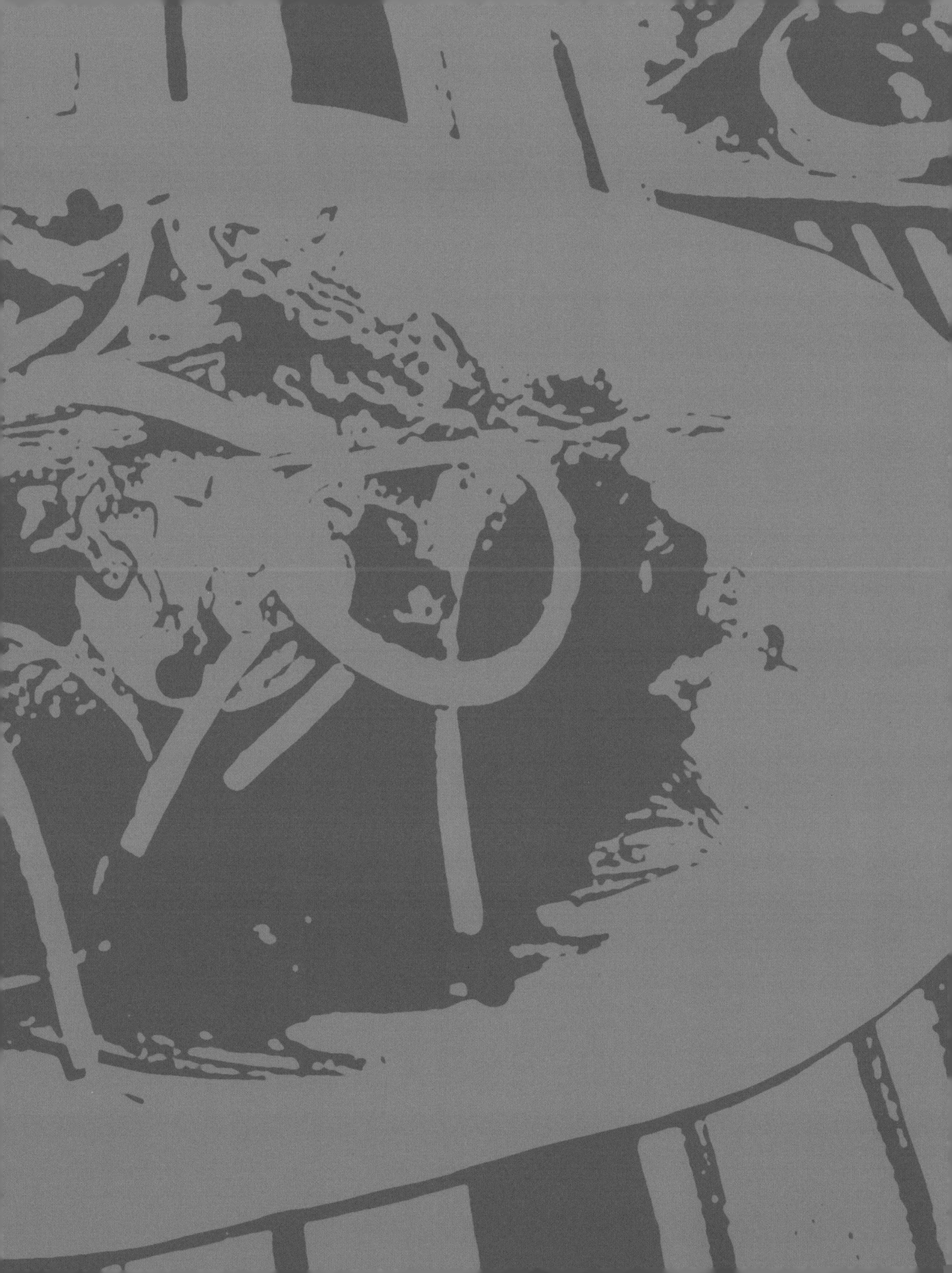

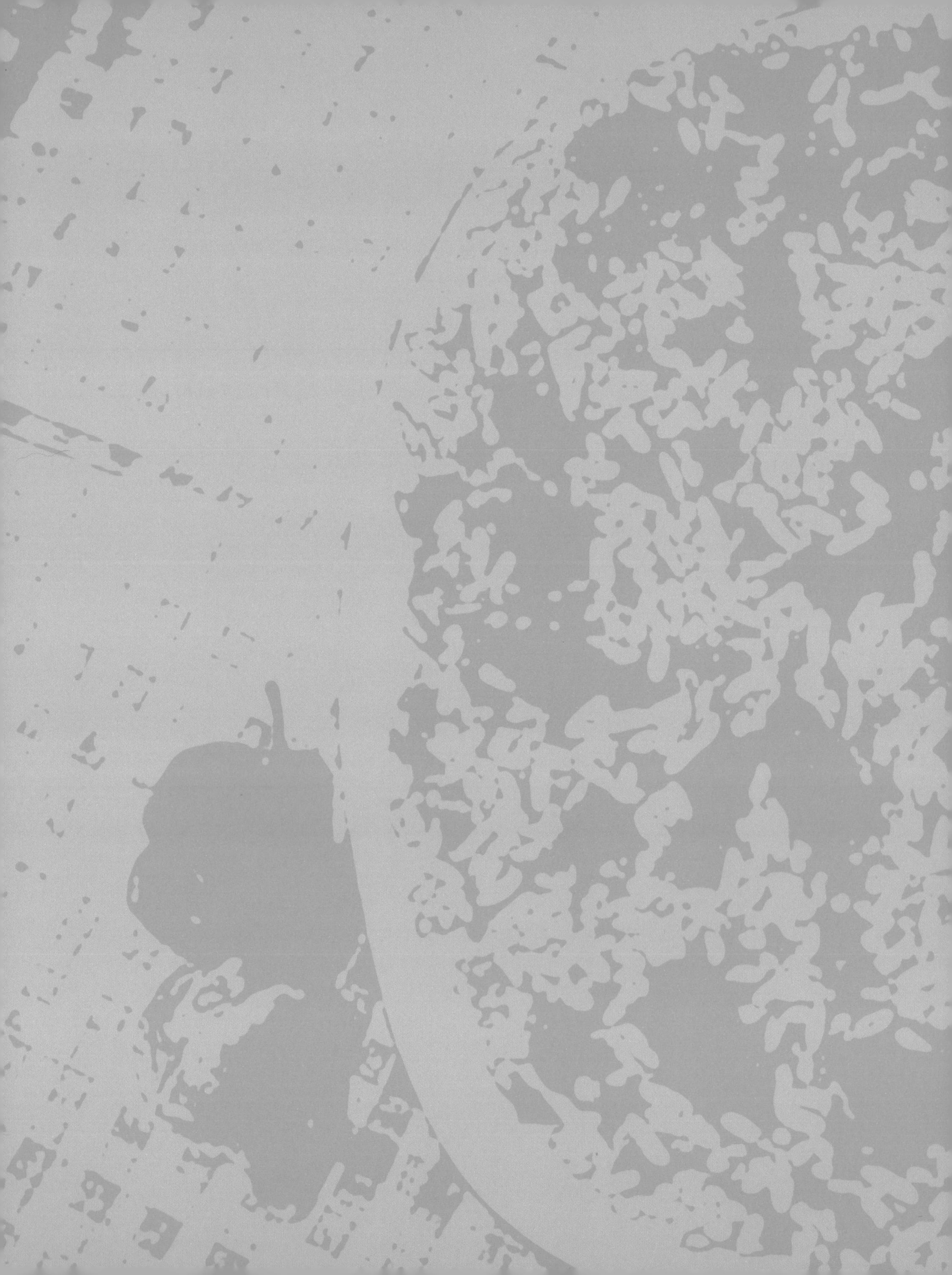

# SIDE DISHES

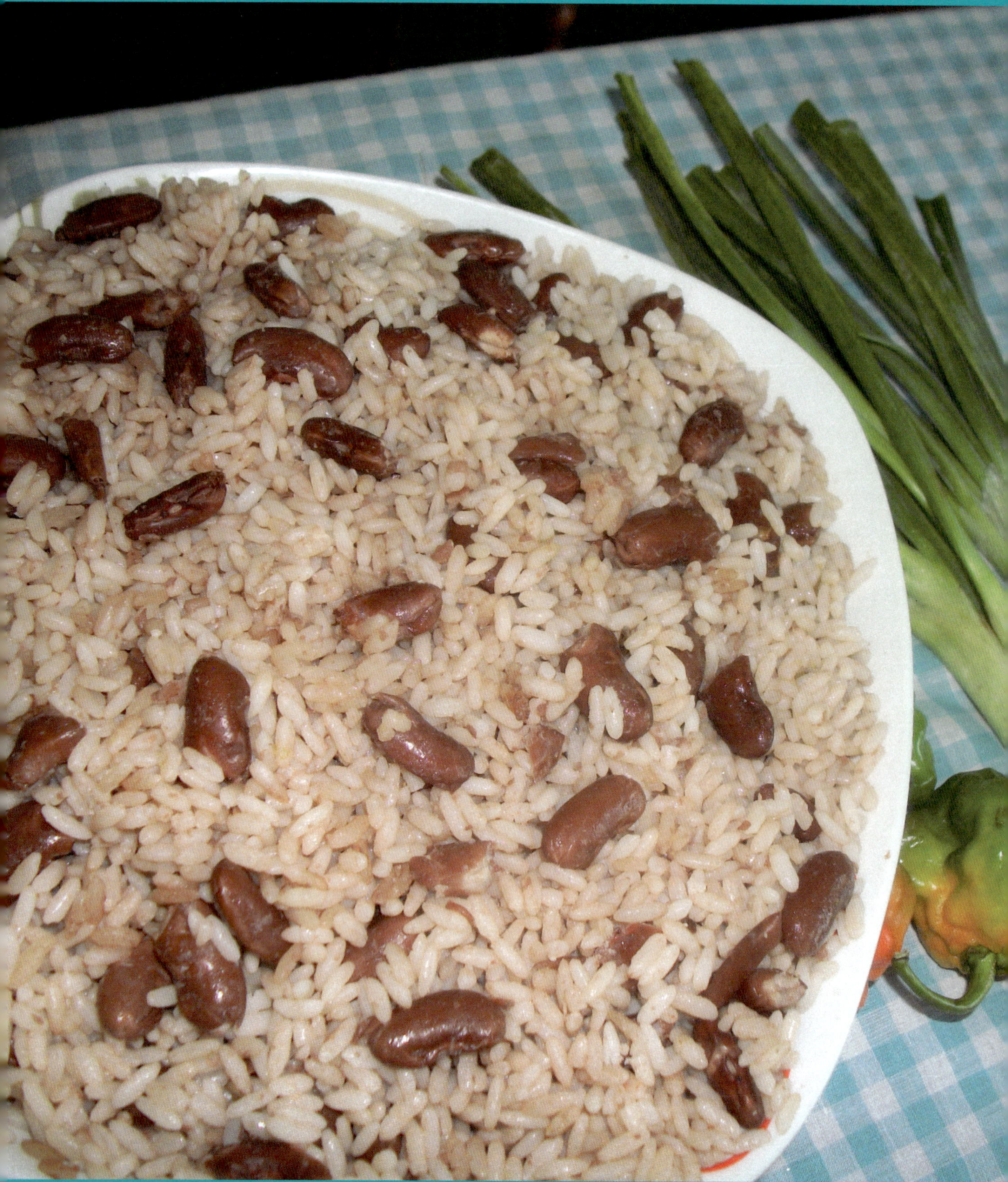

# RICE AND PEAS

| | | |
|---|---|---|
| 12 ozs. | Red (kidney) beans | 350 g. |
| 2 lbs. | Rice | 1 kg. |
| 1 (large) | Coconut | 1 (large) |
| 1 tbsp. | Salt | 1 tbsp. |
| 1 | Onion (med) | 1 |
| 3 | Garlic cloves | 3 |
| 3 | Scallion stalks | 3 |
| 1 tsp. | Thyme | 1 tsp. |
| | Or | |
| ½ tsp. | Thyme (dried) | ½ tsp. |
| 1 | Scotch Bonnet Pepper | 1 |

Crack the shell of the coconut with a hammer, drain the water and remove white coconut meat with a sharp knife. Grate on fine side of grater. Remove juice by mixing in about a quart of water/a liter and squeezing through a strainer.

Rinse peas to remove any foreign matter. In large pot, cover peas with cold water and cook over medium heat, for about an hour.

Peel and coarsely chop onion, peel and crush garlic, and peel and slice scallion including the green tops. Add coconut cream, salt, onion, garlic, scallion, thyme and whole pepper to pot. Continue cooking until peas are tender, and a custard forms. Add rice, stir with a kitchen fork and cover. Turn flame down to low and cook until all water has evaporated and rice is tender. During this time **do not stir**. If rice is not yet cooked, add about ½ cup/125ml water to pot, cover and continue steaming. Check again to see if rice is tender. When cooked, remove pepper from pot.

Yield: About 12 cups

Note- A 13-oz. can of coconut cream can be substituted for the fresh coconut. Add enough water to make up to 4 cups.

SIDE DISHES

# FESTIVAL

| 2 cups  | All-purpose flour | 225 g  |
|---------|-------------------|--------|
| 2/3 cup | Yellow cornmeal   | 150 g  |
| 3 tsp.  | Baking Powder     | 3 tsp. |
| ½ cup   | Brown Sugar       | 120 g. |
|         | Dash of Salt      |        |
| 1 cup   | Water             | 250 ml |
|         | Oil for Frying    |        |

In medium bowl, sift flour and baking powder together. Add cornmeal, sugar and salt. Add water and mix thoroughly. Cover bowl and leave at room temperature for about 20 minutes. In skillet, heat about a ½ inch of oil. Shape small pieces of the dough into an oblong shape. Fry in oil on both sides till golden-brown and cooked all the way through. Drain on absorbent paper.

Makes 16.

# YAM SOUFFLE

| | | |
|---|---|---|
| 2 lbs. | Yam(Yellow or White) | 1kg |
| | Salt | |
| ¼ cup | Butter | 60 g. |
| 1 cup | Milk | 250 ml. |
| 2 | Scallion stalks | 2 |
| 1 | Onion (sm.) | 1 |
| 1 tsp. | Chopped Chives | 1 tsp. |
| 1 tsp. | Rosemary | 1 tsp |
| 1 tsp. | White Pepper | 1 tsp. |
| | Or | |
| ½ tsp. | Hot pepper sauce | ½ tsp. |
| 2 | Eggs (large) | 2 |

**PREHEAT OVEN TO 350°F.**

Bring about 1 quart/liter of water with 2 tsp. of salt to a boil. Peel the yam, cut into chunks and add to boiling water. While yam cooks, peel and thinly slice scallion and peel and chop onion finely. When yam is fork-tender, drain. Mash in large bowl and mix in butter, milk, scallion, onion, chives, rosemary and white pepper or hot pepper sauce.

In small bowl, whip eggs with a hand mixer till very light and pale, about 4 minutes. Fold into yam mixture carefully but thoroughly. Pour into a greased 1 ½ -qt./1 ½ -liter baking dish, mark top decoratively with a fork and place in preheated oven. Bake for 20-25 minutes. Serve hot.

8 servings.

SIDE DISHES

# SWEET POTATO CASSEROLE

| | | |
|---|---|---|
| 3 lbs. | Sweet Potato | 1 ½ kg. |
| 1 qt. | Orange Juice | 1 liter |
| ¼ cup | Butter | 60 g. |
| ½ cup | Brown Sugar | 120 g. |
| 1 tsp. | Grated Nutmeg | 1 tsp. |

Wash and scrub sweet potatoes thoroughly. Wrap each potato in aluminium foil and place in oven for about 45 minutes or until half-baked. Remove from oven and cool completely.

Peel and slice sweet potatoes. Put down a single layer in a 3-qt. /3 liter baking dish, sprinkle with brown sugar and grated nutmeg. Lay down two more layers, in the same manner. Dot the top with the butter. Pour the orange juice into the dish slowly from the side, making sure that all the slices are covered. Place in 350 F oven and bake uncovered for 45-50 minutes. Serve hot.

12 servings.

# FRIED BAMMY

It is best to purchase bammies as it would be extremely time- consuming to make them from scratch.

Grated cassava is the main ingredient in this flat, unleavened bread. Bammy is sold in various sizes ranging from the large size which is about 6 inches in diameter to smaller individual and cocktail sizes and makes the perfect pairing with Escovitch fish.

| | | |
|---|---|---|
| 2 lge or 8 sm | Bammies | 2 lge or 8 sm |
| 1 cup | Milk | 250 ml |
| | Cooking Oil | |

If using regular-sized bammies, cut each in 8 triangles. Pour milk into a shallow dish. Soak for about 5 minutes on one side, then turn over and soak on the other side for a further 5 minutes.

In a large skillet pour cooking oil to a depth of about ¼ "or 5 mm. Heat oil till the surface ripples slightly and place bammies in skillet in a single layer. Fry on each side till golden and drain on absorbent paper.

Serve hot.

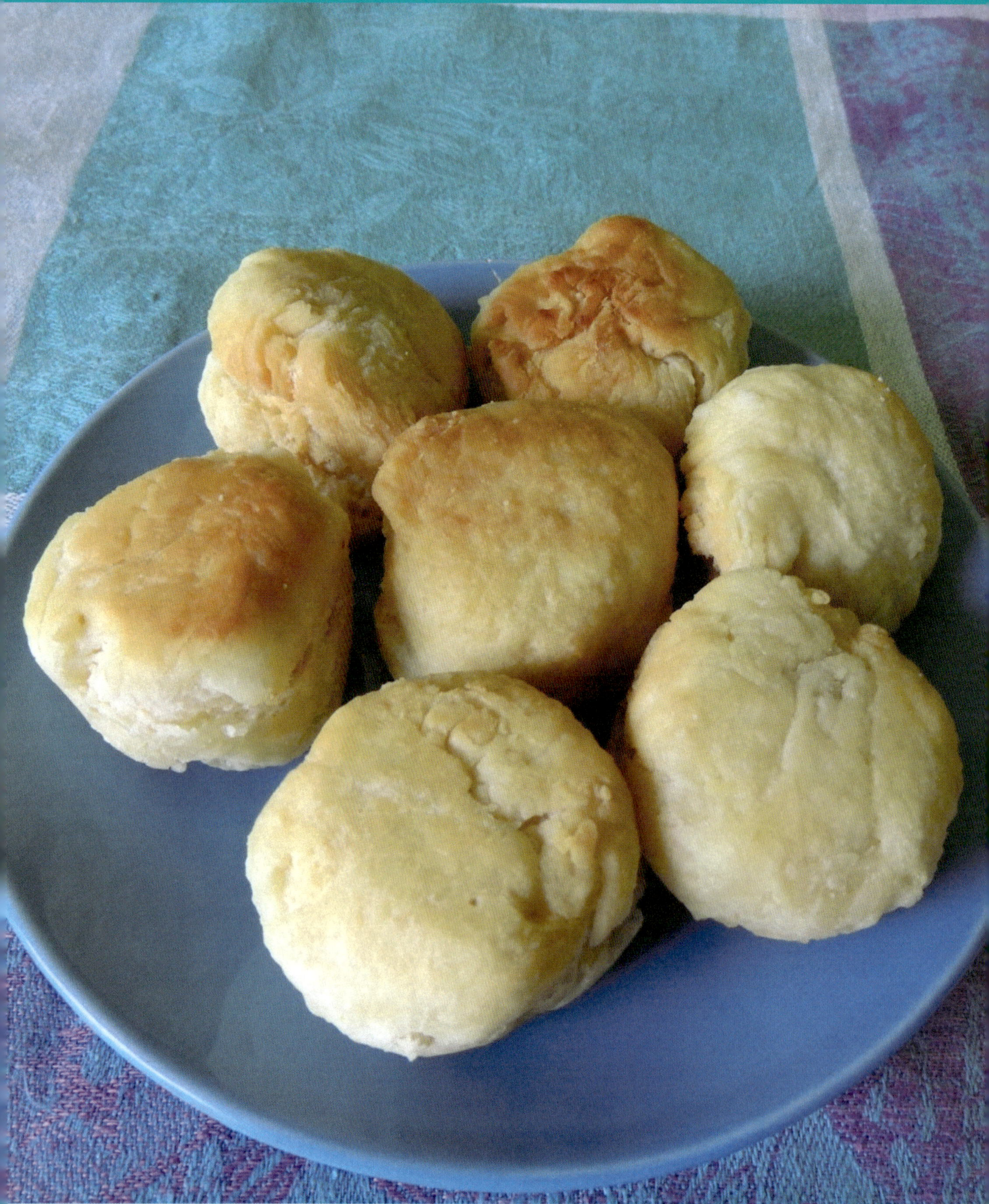

# FRIED DUMPLINGS

| | | |
|---|---|---|
| 2 cups | All-purpose flour | 225 g. |
| 3 tsp. | Baking Powder | 3 tsp. |
| Dash | Salt | Dash |
| 1 tbsp. | Sugar | 1 tbsp. |
| | Water | |
| | Oil for Frying | |

In medium bowl, sift together all dry ingredients. Add enough water to make a soft dough. Place skillet on high heat and pour in oil to about ¼ of an inch. Dust palms with flour, pull off small pieces of dough and shape into round dumplings. When there are small ripples on the surface of the oil, start frying dumplings. Lower heat to medium and continue cooking until done all the way through, turning as necessary.

Serve hot.

Makes about 12.

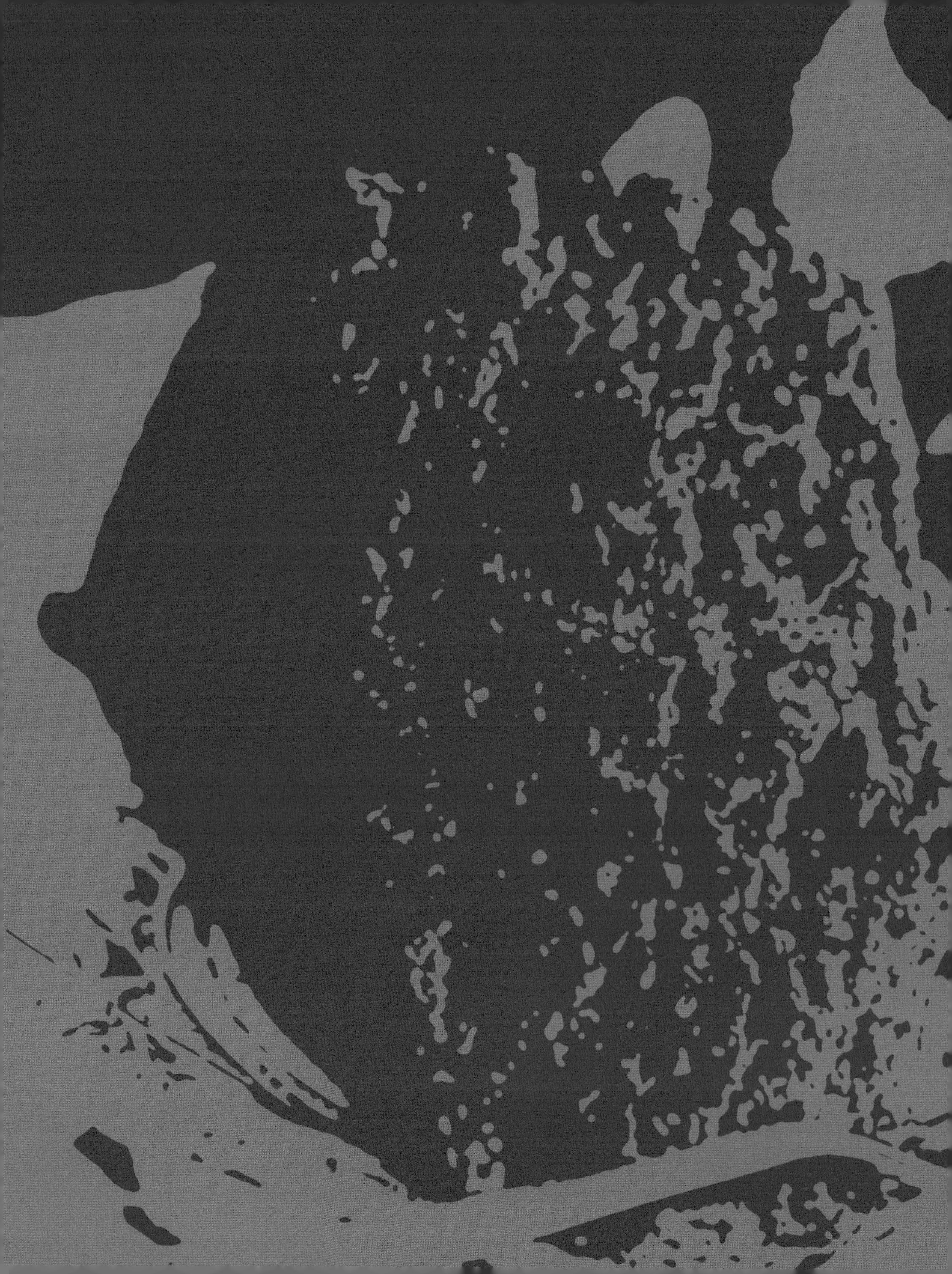

# SWEETS AND DESSERTS

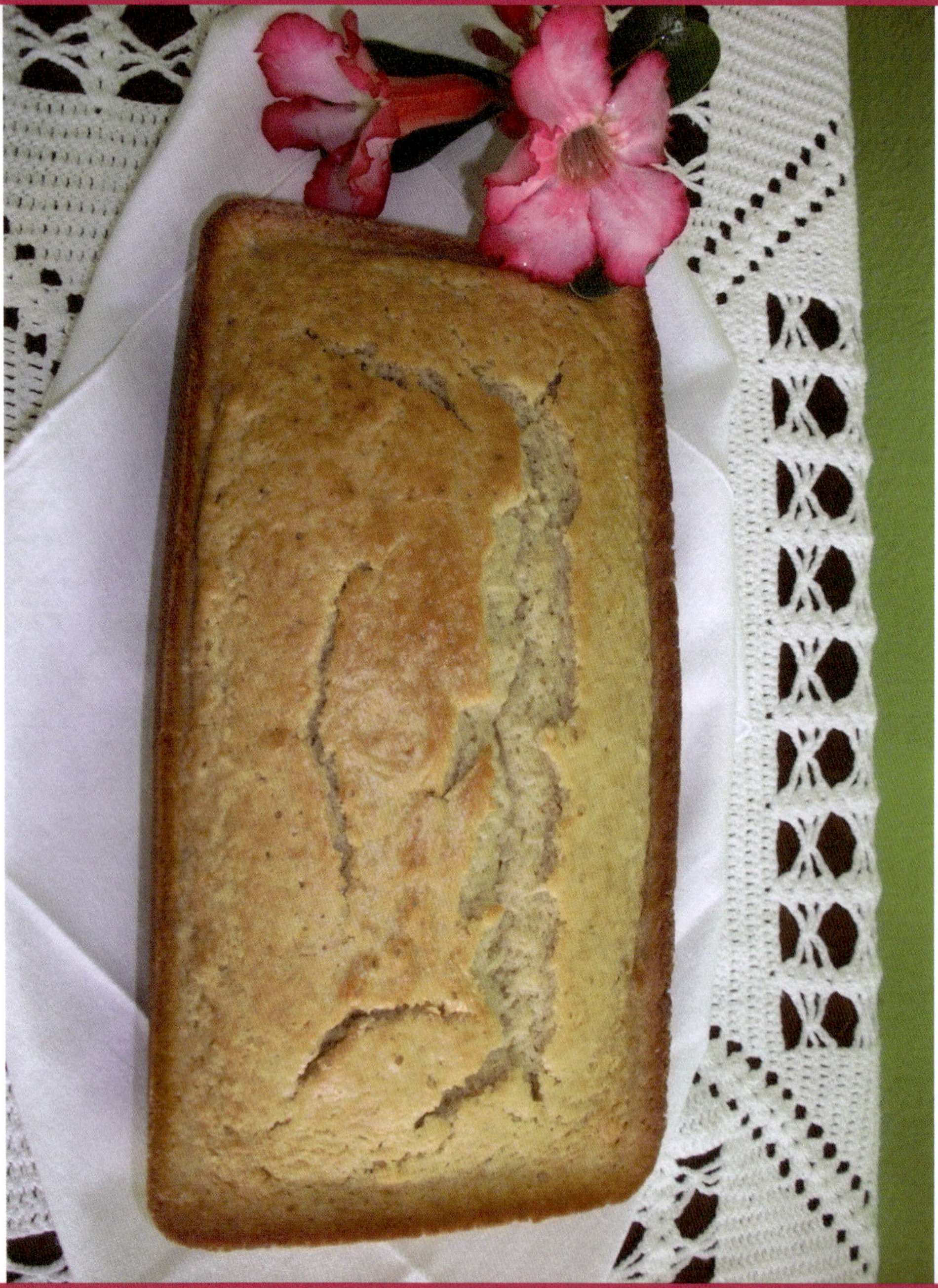

# COCONUT BREAD

| | | |
|---|---|---|
| 2 | Eggs | 2 |
| ½ cup | Butter | 120 g |
| 1 cup | Granulated Sugar | 225 g |
| 1 tsp. | Vanilla | 1 tsp. |
| 1 tsp. | Rum | 1 tsp. |
| ½ tsp | Grated Nutmeg | ½ tsp. |
| 2 cups | All-purpose flour | 225 g. |
| 3 tsp. | Baking Powder | 3 tsp. |
| 1 cup | Grated Coconut | 250 ml |
| ¾ cup | Milk | 180 ml |
| ½ cup | Raisins | 90 g. |
| | Corn Syrup | |

Preheat oven to 325°F.

Sift flour and baking powder together in large bowl and set aside. In small bowl, combine butter, eggs, sugar, rum, vanilla and nutmeg and cream together until smooth and light with a mixer. Add butter mixture to flour mixture along with coconut, milk and raisins. Mix for no more than 2 minutes. Pour into greased loaf tin and place in oven. Bake for about 50 minutes. Bread is done when a knife or skewer inserted comes out clean. Cool slightly before removing from pan. Cool completely. Brush with corn syrup.

8-10 servings.

To help prevent raisins from sinking to the bottom, wet them and coat with flour before mixing into batter.

Fresh grated coconut would be the first choice but desiccated, grated coconut can also be used.

# BANANA BREAD

| | | |
|---|---|---|
| 2 | Eggs | 2 |
| ½ cup | Butter | 115 g |
| 1 cup | Brown Sugar | 225 g. |
| ½ tsp. | Grated Nutmeg | ½ tsp |
| ½ tsp. | Cinnamon | ½ tsp |
| 1 tsp. | Vanilla | 1 tsp. |
| 2 cups | All-purpose flour | 225 g. |
| 3 tbsps. | Baking Powder | 3 tbsps. |
| 3 | Very Ripe Bananas | 3 |
| ½ cup | Orange Juice | 125 ml. |
| ½ cup | Raisins | 90 g. |
| | Fruit Jelly | |

Preheat oven to 325°F. Grease loaf tin and set aside.

In large bowl, sift flour and baking powder together. Peel and blend bananas. In small bowl, combine eggs, butter, sugar, vanilla, nutmeg and cinnamon. With a mixer, cream until smooth and light. Add butter mixture to flour mixture along with bananas, juice and raisins. Mix for no more than two minutes. Pour into prepared tin and bake for about 50 minutes. Bread is done when a knife or skewer inserted comes out clean. Cool slightly and remove from pan. Cool completely.

Beat jelly with fork until it is spreadable. Spread over top of banana bread.

8-10 servings.

# GIZZARDAS "PINCH-ME-ROUND"

| | | |
|---|---|---|
| 1 | Coconut (large) | 1 |
| | Or | |
| 3 cups | Grated desiccated coconut | 750 ml |
| 1 ½ cups | Granulated Sugar | 335 g. |
| ¾ cup | Water | 200 ml |
| ½ tsp | Vanilla | ½ tsp |
| ½ tsp | Almond Essence | ½ tsp |
| 2 ½ cups | All-purpose flour | 280 g |
| ½ cup | Shortening | 115 g |
| Dash | Salt | Dash |
| | Ice-cold water | |
| | Glazed Cherries | |

Break coconut open with a hammer and remove flesh with a sharp knife. Peel away brown skin. Grate in the medium side of grater. In a small heavy pot, mix sugar and water and bring to boil. Boil for 10 minutes. Add the coconut and flavourings and mix well. Set aside to cool.

Sift together flour and salt in a medium bowl. Cut in the shortening until mixture resembles fine breadcrumbs. Add enough ice-cold water to make a dough. Sprinkle counter with flour and roll out dough to a 1/8" thickness. Using a round 4"/9 cm cutter, cut circles from the dough. Make little pinches all around the circle so that you end up with a little "plate" with sides that go up about ½ "/1 cm. Fill each one with coconut mixture and place cherry quarter on top of each. Place on a greased cookie sheet and place in a preheated 350 F oven. Bake for 15-20 minutes or until the crust is golden. With a spatula, remove from baking sheet while still hot. Cool before serving.

Makes about 18.

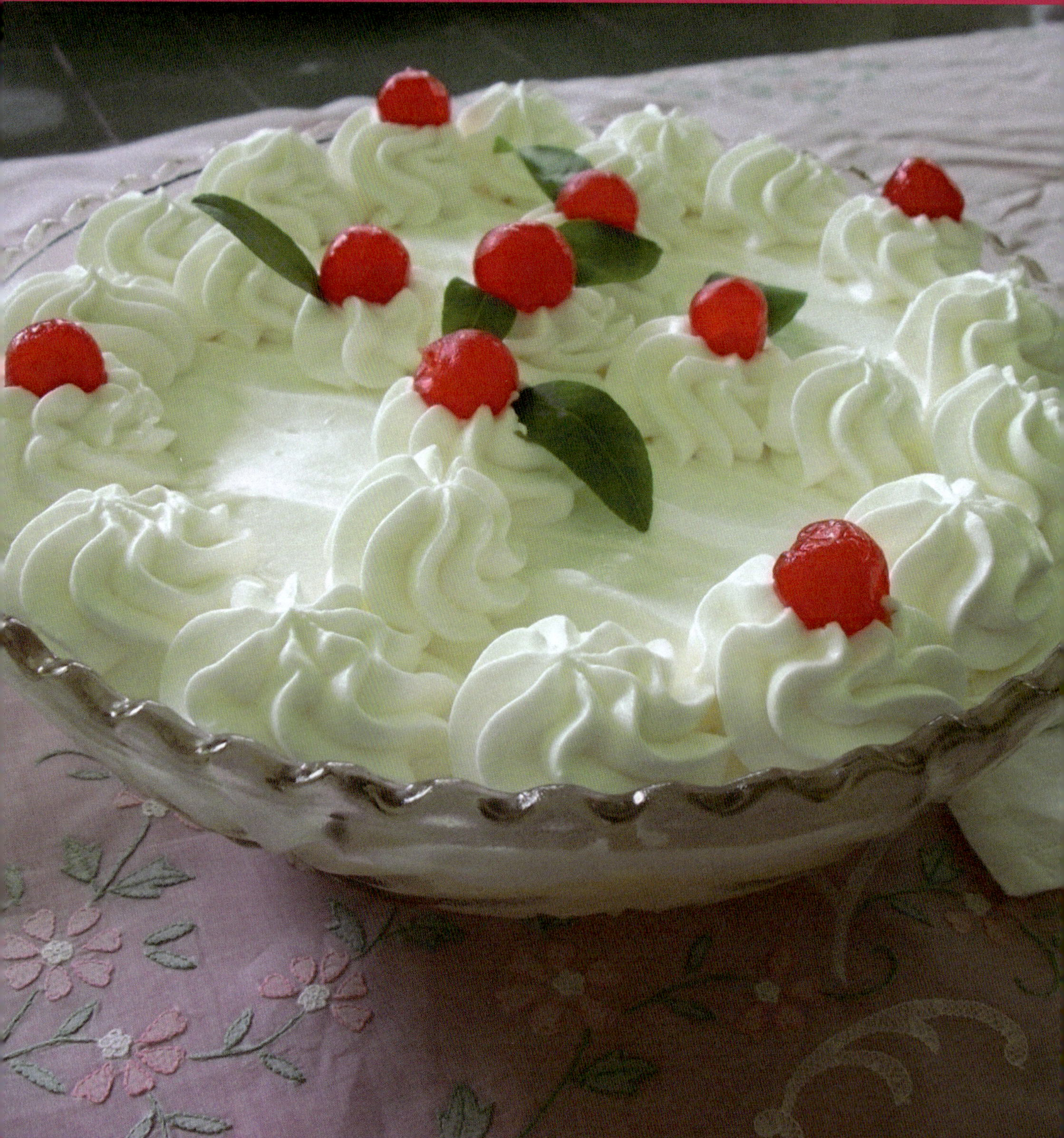

# RUM TRIFLE

| | | |
|---|---|---|
| 1 | 9" Sponge Layer | 1 |
| ¼ cup | Jam | 60 ml |
| 1 oz. | Jamaica Dark Rum | 30 ml |
| 1 cup | Fruit (canned or fresh) | 250 ml |
| 2 cups | Milk | 500 ml |
| 4 | Egg Yolks | 4 |
| ½ cup | Sugar | 125 g |
| 3 heaping tbsps. | Cornstarch | 3 heaping tbsps. |
| 1 tsp | vanilla | 1 tsp. |
| 1 cup | whipping cream | 250 ml |
| 2 tbsp. | Icing Sugar | 2 tbsp. |
| | Maraschino Cherries | |
| | Slivered Almonds | |
| | Or | |
| | Toasted Grated Coconut | |

Select a glass or crystal dish that is as attractive as you can find.

Place layer of sponge cake in the bottom of dish and sprinkle with rum.

Spread with guava or strawberry jam. Choose any combination of fruit such as pineapple, mango, mandarin oranges, peach, strawberry or raspberry and spread over sponge cake. Set aside.

In a heavy saucepan, whisk the milk, egg yolks, sugar, cornstarch and vanilla. Bring to a gentle boil stirring constantly to avoid all lumps. Remove from heat and pour over the cake and fruit. Allow the custard to cool completely.

In small mixing bowl beat cream and icing sugar together till soft peaks form. Do not overbeat. Cover cooled custard completely and pipe decoratively with a piping bag and a star tip. Decorate with maraschino cherries and almonds or toasted coconut. Chill thoroughly before serving.

Makes 10-12 servings.

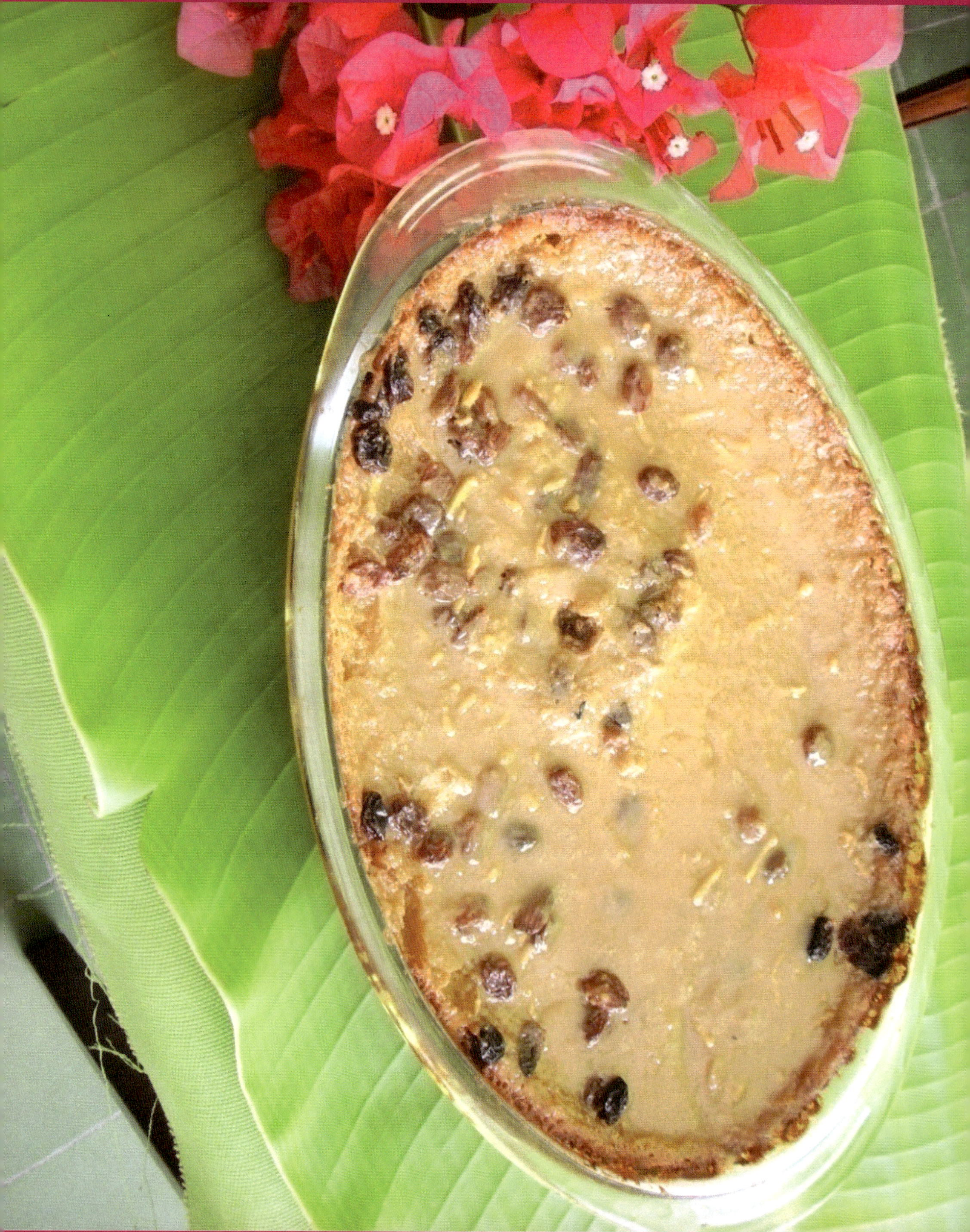

# SWEET POTATO PUDDING

Use fresh nutmeg and grate just before adding to mixture.

| | | |
|---|---|---|
| 1 lb. | Sweet Potato | 450 g |
| 2 cups | Brown Sugar | 450 g |
| 1 ½ cup | All-purpose Flour | 170 g |
| 1 tsp | Salt | 1 tsp |
| ½ cup | Milk | 120 ml |
| 1 | Egg (slightly beaten) | 1 |
| 1 | Coconut (small) | 1 |
| 1 heaping tsp | Nutmeg (grated) | 1 heaping tsp |
| 1 tbsp | Vanilla | 1 tbsp |
| ½ cup | Raisins | 75 g |

Crack coconut open with a hammer, drain water and husk out the flesh with a small, sharp knife. Grate on the medium side of the grater. Mix with about 2 cups/500ml of water and squeeze through a strainer. Measure coconut juice to 2 ½ cups/625ml and set aside.

Wash, peel and grate potato on medium side of the grater. Set aside.

Preheat oven to 350°F. Grease 9" round pan very well and set aside.

In large mixing bowl, combine all ingredients, and stir well. Mixture will be watery. Pour mixture into pan and place in oven for 90 minutes. The top will be soft when completely baked. Cool completely before serving.

15-18 servings.

If fresh coconut is not used a 5 oz. can of unsweetened coconut cream or a packet of coconut powder can be substituted. Add enough water to make up to 2 ½ cups.

SWEETS AND DESSERTS

# FRUIT SALAD

| 2 lbs | Watermelon | 1 kg |
| --- | --- | --- |
| 1 | Pineapple (med) | 1 |
| 4 | Oranges or Ortaniques | 4 |
| 1 | Papaya(sm) | 1 |
| 2 | Mangoes (large) | 2 |
| 1 cup | Strawberry Syrup | 250 ml |
| | Optional | |
| | Maraschino Cherries | |

Cut watermelon out of the rind, cut in large pieces and remove the seeds, then cut into 1"/2 cm cubes.

Remove the top leaves of the pineapple and peel. Quarter and remove the fibrous core. Cut into 1"/2cm cubes.

With a sharp knife, remove the skin and white pith from oranges. Pull segments apart and remove membranes.

Peel papaya, halve and remove seeds. Cut in ½ "/1cm cubes.

Peel mangoes, and cut flesh away from seeds. Cut into ½"/1cm cubes.

Combine all the fruit in a large attractive bowl. Pour syrup over fruit and combine gently. Chill thoroughly. Decorate with maraschino cherries, if desired.

Serves 12.

# MATRIMONY

| | | |
|---|---|---|
| 4 | Starapples | 4 |
| 2 | Navel Oranges | 2 |
| ¼ cup | Condensed Milk | 60 ml |
| ¼ tsp | Nutmeg (grated) | ¼ tsp |

Halve Starapples and remove the stringy core. Scoop out the pulp. Remove seeds from pulp. With a sharp knife, remove skin and pith from oranges. Separate segments and remove the membranes.

Fold together Starapples, orange segments, condensed milk and freshly grated nutmeg. Chill thoroughly. Serve in glass bowls and decorate with citrus leaves, if possible.

Serves 4

SWEETS AND DESSERTS

# OTAHEITI APPLE PIE

|  | Shortcrust Pastry (p. 15) |  |
|---|---|---|
| 6 cups | Otaheiti Apple Slices | 1 ½ liters |
| ¾ cup | Granulated Sugar | 180 g. |
| 3 tbsp | Lime Juice | 3 tbsp |
| ½ cup | Cornstarch | 60 g |
|  | Milk |  |
|  | Granulated Sugar |  |

Wash apples and remove stem and bud ends. **Do not peel.** Halve and remove seeds. Slice. In large pot, combine apple slices, sugar, lime juice and 1 cup/250 ml water. Cook on medium heat till apples are soft and pink. Dissolve cornstarch in a little water and stir well into apples. Remove pot from heat and set aside to cool completely.

Preheat oven to 375°F. Divide the Shortcrust dough a two-thirds portion and a one-third portion. On a floured surface, roll out the larger portion to a 12- inch circle and line a 9-inch pie pan. Pour in cooled filling. Roll out the smaller portion to a 10-inch circle and cut out several small slits or decorative shapes. Lay over apples, tuck under edges and crimp. With a pastry brush, brush topcrust with milk and sprinkle with granulated sugar. Place in oven and bake for 40 to 45 minutes. Cool before serving.

10 servings.

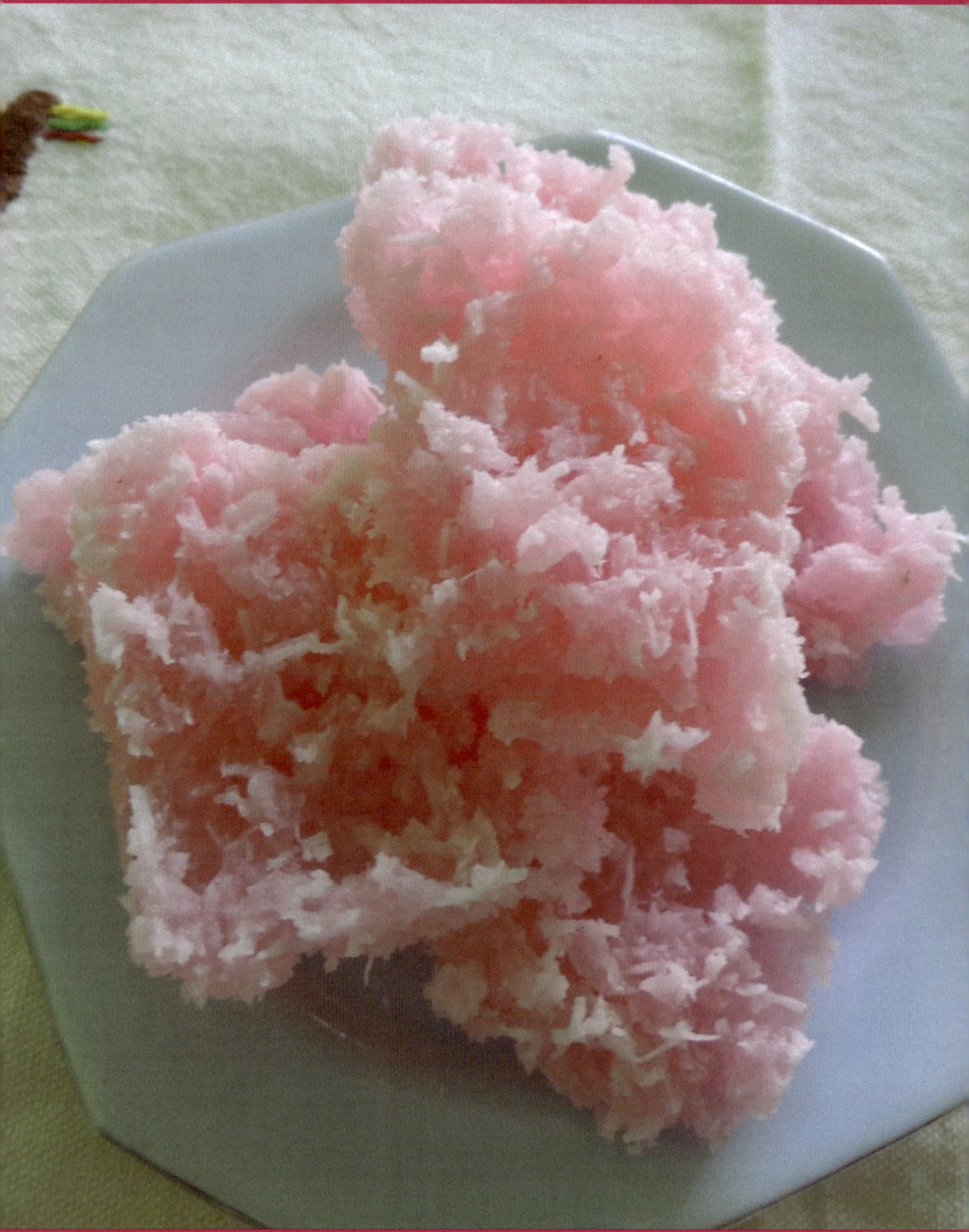

# GRATER CAKE

| | | |
|---|---|---|
| 1 | Coconut (med) | 1 |
| 2 cups | Granulated Sugar | 450 g |
| ¾ cup | Water | 180 ml |
| ½ tsp | Vanilla | ½ tsp |
| ½ tsp | Almond Extract | ½ tsp |

Break coconut and drain water. With a small, sharp knife remove coconut from shell. Using knife, remove brown skin. Grate on medium side of grater.

In medium, heavy saucepan, bring water and sugar to a boil. Boil for 5-6 minutes. Add coconut and flavourings and stir well. Continue cooking on medium-high heat for 8 minutes, stirring occasionally. For the next 2 minutes, stir constantly. Mixture should reach 220 F on a candy thermometer. Turn out on **wet** plate or cookie sheet. Spread quickly into an even ¾" layer. With sharp knife cut into 2" squares. Cool completely then lift squares off plate with a spatula. Store in an air-tight tin.

Yields 18 squares.

If desired, 3-4 drops of red food colouring can be added to boiling sugar and water to produce delicate pink grater cakes.

SWEETS AND DESSERTS

# BULLAS

| | | |
|---|---|---|
| 2 ½ cups | All-purpose flour | 280 g |
| 2/3 cup | Brown Sugar | 150 g |
| ½ cup | Water | 120 ml |
| 2 tbsp | Margarine or Shortening | 2 tbsp |
| 2 tbsp | Molasses | 2 tbsp |
| 1 tsp | Baking Soda | 1 tsp |
| 1 oz | Ginger Root | 30 g |
| | Or | |
| | 1 tbsp. ground Ginger | |
| ¼ tsp | Cinnamon | ¼ tsp |
| ¼ tsp | Mixed Spice | ¼ tsp |

Sift together once the flour, baking soda, cinnamon, mixed spice and ground ginger, if used. If using fresh ginger, wash, peel and juice with the water and set aside.

Preheat oven to 350°F. In a small heavy pan, combine sugar, molasses and plain water or the ginger juice, if used. Mix all thoroughly and simmer gently over low heat until the sugar is melted. Remove from heat. Cool completely. Add syrup along with margarine or shortening to flour mixture. Mix well with spoon, then turn out and knead lightly on a floured surface. Sprinkle with flour and using a rolling pin, roll out to a ½" thickness. Cut out 4"/ 10cm circles, till all the dough is used up. Place circles on a greased cookie sheet and bake in oven for 20-25 minutes. Lift off sheet while still hot and allow to cool.

Recipe can be doubled.

Makes 9.

# PLANTAIN TARTS

| | | |
|---|---|---|
| 3 | Ripe Plantains (large) | 3 |
| ¾ cup | Sugar (White or Brown) | 175 g |
| 1 tsp | Vanilla | 1 tsp |
| ½ tsp | Almond Essence (if desired) | ½ tsp |
| 4-5 drops | Red Food Colouring | 4-5 drops |
| 3 ½ cup | All-purpose Flour | 400 g |
| ¾ cup | Shortening | 150 g |
| ½ cup | Granulated Sugar | 105 g |
| ½ tsp | Salt | ½ tsp |
| | Ice-cold Water | |
| 1 | Egg | 1 |

Select very ripe plantains with dark spots. Peel and cut each in 3-4 pieces. Place in medium saucepan, and cover with water. Bring to a boil and cook until plantain is tender. Drain. Either mash with a fork or place in blender and process at medium speed. Add sugar, vanilla, almond flavouring and enough colouring to give a delicate pink and mix thoroughly. Cool completely and set aside.

Preheat oven to 400° F. Sift flour and salt together twice. Add granulated sugar. Work shortening into flour mixture with fingers until it resembles breadcrumbs. Add enough ice-cold water for dough to hold together. Roll out on a floured surface to a 1/8 "/3mm thickness and cut 5" /12 cm circles. Place about 3 tablespoons of plantain filling in centre. Fold over and crimp edges with a fork. Place on a greased baking sheet. Beat egg slightly. Brush top of each tart with egg and sprinkle with brown sugar before placing in oven for about 25 minutes or until tarts are golden-brown. Cool before serving.

Makes 12 tarts.

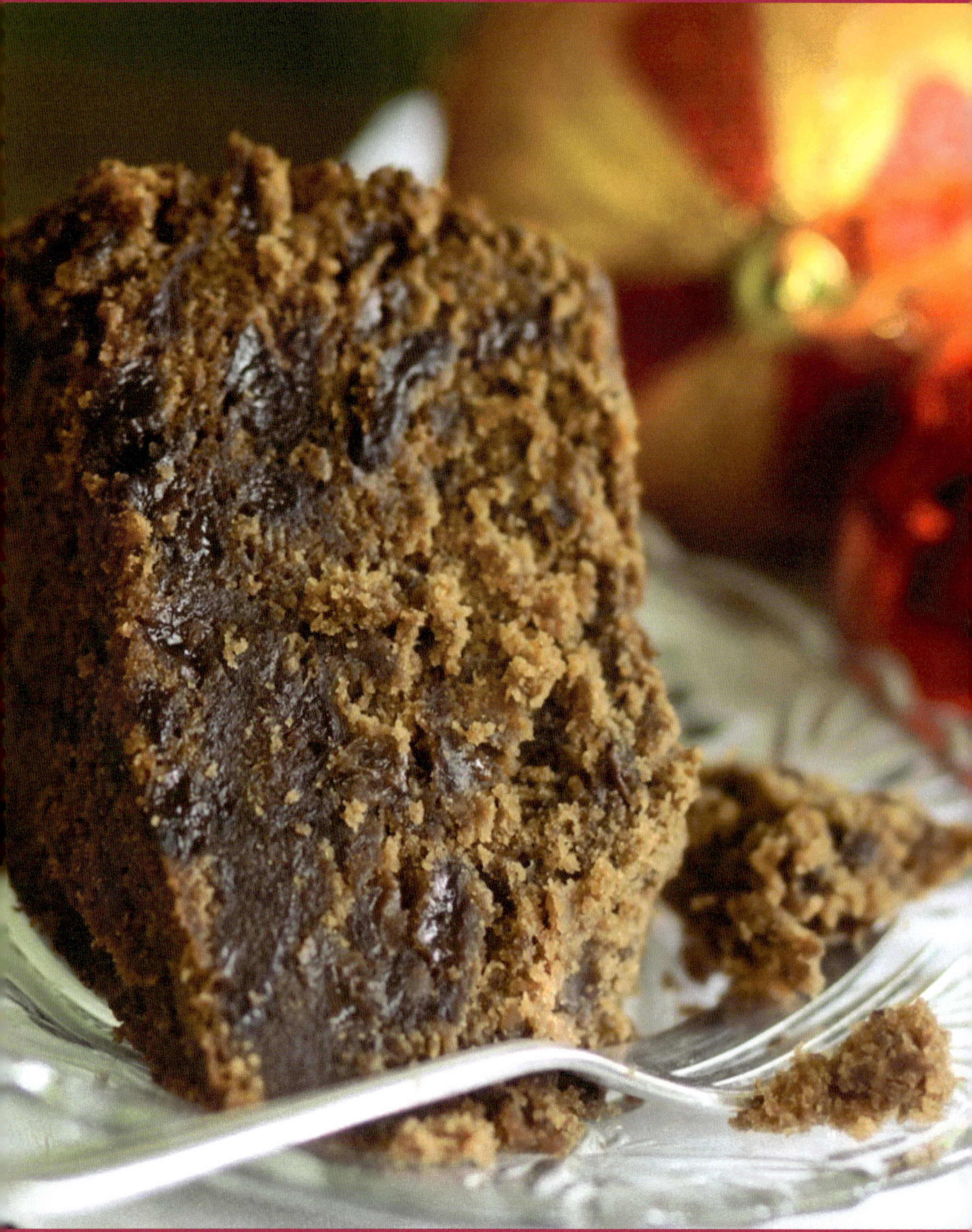

# CHRISTMAS FRUITCAKE

| | | |
|---|---|---|
| 1 lb | Raisins | 450 g |
| 1 cup | Red Wine | 250 ml |
| ¼ cup | Rum | 60 ml |
| 8 ozs | Prunes | 225 g |
| 4 ozs | Glazed Cherries | 110 g |
| 1 oz | Mixed Peel | 30 g |
| 1 cup | Butter | 225 g |
| 1 cup | Brown Sugar | 225 g |
| 4 | Eggs | 4 |
| 1 tsp | Vanilla | 1 tsp |
| ½ tsp | Almond Essence | ½ tsp |
| ½ tsp | Orange Flavouring | ½ tsp |
| 1 tbsp | Cherry Brandy | 1 tbsp |
| 2 cups | Flour | 225 g |
| 1 cup | Pineapple Juice | 240 ml |
| | Caramel Colouring | |

At least the day before, but for as long as a year before, place raisins in saucepan and pour the wine over. Cover and boil gently over a medium heat, until raisins plump. Cool completely, place in a glass or ceramic jar with a tight cover and pour in rum. Cover and set aside.

Chop prunes and cherries and set aside. Mince peel finely and set aside. Sift flour and set aside. Grease and line with parchment paper a 9" baking pan and set aside. Preheat oven to 300°F. In mixing bowl combine butter, sugar, eggs and all flavourings. Beat on high speed with electric mixer till high and light. Add flour and stir in until just blended. Add all the fruits and pineapple juice and stir in till just blended. Add enough caramel colouring to give a dark brown colour. Pour into baking pan, cover and seal pan with aluminium foil and place in oven. Bake for about 2 hours. Cake is done when knife comes out almost clean. Cool overnight.

Makes 4 ½ lb/ 2 kg cake

Serves about 20.

# DRINKS

DRINKS

# GINGER BEER

| 1 ½ cup | Brown Sugar | 350 g |
| 4 | Limes | 4 |
| 4 ozs. | Jamaica Ginger | 120 g. |
| 2 quarts | Water | 2 liters |

In a small heavy pot, stir together sugar and 2 cups/ 500 ml water. Bring to a boil and simmer for 5 minutes. Remove from heat and cool completely. Set aside.

Wash and halve limes. Juice and set aside.

Wash thoroughly and peel ginger root with a small, sharp knife. Either grate on the medium side of a grater or blend on high speed with 2 cups of water in an electric blender. With either method of grating, add enough water to make up to 6 cups/1 ½ liters. Add lime juice to ginger mixture. Strain through a fine strainer, pressing down with the back of a spoon. Add sugar syrup and stir. Chill. Serve in tall glasses over ice. Decorate with lime slices, if desired.

Makes about 2 qts/2liters

Another version can be made using granulated sugar. Add 2-3 drops of red food colouring.

# SORREL

| | | |
|---|---|---|
| 1 lb | Sorrel (picked) | 450 g. |
| 3 qts | Water | 3 liters |
| 1 tsp | Whole Pimento Seeds | 1 tsp. |
| 4 | Limes | 4 |
| 1 cup | Granulated Sugar | 225 g. |
| ½ cup | Jamaica Rum | 125 ml |

Wash sorrel thoroughly. In non-metallic or stainless steel pot combine water, sorrel and pimento. Boil for 15 minutes, covered. In the meantime, cut limes in half and juice. Set aside. Remove sorrel from heat and cool. Strain but allow the pimento to remain. Add lime juice, sugar and rum and stir well to dissolve sugar. Taste and if desired, add more sugar. Pour into bottles and cover tightly and refrigerate. Pimento seeds will rise to the top. Sorrel will keep for several weeks.

Makes 3 qts/3 liters.

DRINKS

# SHANDY

Beer
Ginger Beer

Use equal parts of both. Make sure both are chilled. Pour ginger beer into tall glass half-filled with ice, then slowly pour in an equal amount of beer. Stir lightly and serve immediately.

# BLUE MOUTAIN COFFEE FLOAT

| | | |
|---|---|---|
| 1 qt. | Blue Mountain Coffee | 1 lt. |
| ½ cup | Evaporated Milk | 125 ml |
| ½ cup | Brown Sugar | 120 g |
| 4 scoops | Chocolate Ice Cream | 4 scoops |
| | Whipped Cream | |
| Optional: | | |
| 4 ozs | Jamaican Rum | 4 ozs |

Brew 4 level tablespoons ground Blue Mountain Coffee to make 1 quart. Add the evaporated milk and sugar, stirring well. Allow to cool completely. In the meantime, chill 4 tall glasses till frosty.

When ready to make the floats, pour coffee into glasses about ¾ full. If desired, pour about an ounce of rum into each glass and stir. Add a scoop of ice cream to each glass and top with a large dollop of whipped cream. Serve with straws.

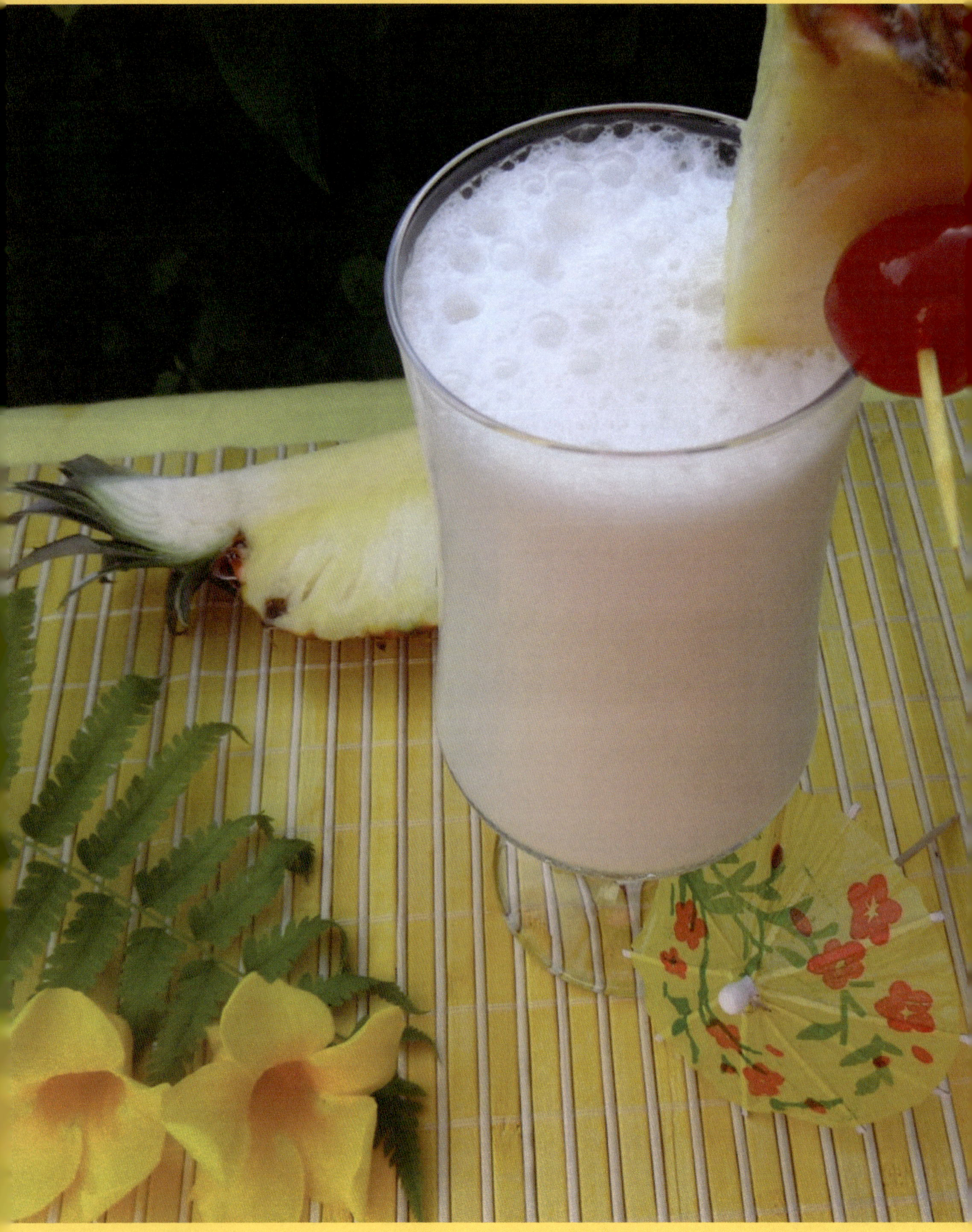

# PINA COLADA

| | | |
|---|---|---|
| 8 ozs. | Coconut Cream( unsweetened) | 240 ml |
| 12 ozs | Unsweetened Pineapple Juice | 375 ml |
| ¼ cup | Jamaican Rum | 60 ml |
| ½ cup | Simple Syrup(p. 99) | 120 ml |
| 8 | Ice Cubes | 8 |
| | Pineapple Sticks | |
| | Maraschino Cherries | |

Chill 2 tall glasses. Shake the can of coconut cream well. Place the first five ingredients in a blender and blend till smooth. Pour into the glasses and decorate with pineapple sticks and cherries. Serve with straws. Makes 2 drinks.

DRINKS

# RUM PUNCH

| | | |
|---|---|---|
| 2 tbsp. | Lime Juice | 2 tbsp. |
| 4 tbsp. | Strawberry Syrup | 4 tbsp. |
| 6 tbsp. | Jamaica Red Rum | 6 tbspl |
| ½ cup | Water | 120 ml |
| | Ice Cubes | |
| | Lime Slices | |
| | Maraschino Cherries | |

Make the 2 tbsp. juice from fresh limes. Strain. Add strawberry syrup, rum and water. Stir. Pour over ice in chilled short glasses. Garnish with lime slices and maraschino cherries.

Makes 2 drinks.

# MANGO LIMEADE

| | | |
|---|---|---|
| ½ cup | Lime Juice | 120 ml |
| 6 cups | Water | 1 ½ liters |
| 1 ½ cup | Granulated Sugar | 350 g |
| 2 cups | Mango Juice | 500 ml |
| | Ice Cubes | |
| | Mango strips | |
| | Maraschino Cherries | |

Halve and juice enough limes to make the ½ cup. In large pitcher combine lime juice, water, sugar and mango juice. Stir until sugar is completely dissolved. Chill completely. Fill tall glasses with ice cubes and pour in limeade. Garnish with strips of fresh or canned mango, if available, and maraschino cherries. Serve immediately.

Makes 2 ½ quarts/liters

# SOURSOP JUICE

The Soursop is also called the sapodilla.

Peel and remove the stem from a large ripe Soursop or several smaller ones. The large black seeds will remain. Place in a large bowl and add 2 quarts/liters of water. Using a potato masher, work the pulp thoroughly. Pour through a large sieve and press down using the back of a large spoon, squeezing out all the liquid. Finish juice either with granulated sugar and 2 or 3 juiced limes or with sweetened condensed milk to taste. This is a matter of personal preference. Chill thoroughly and serve in tall glasses.

Yields about 3 quarts/liters

# LIME SQUASH

| | | |
|---|---|---|
| 2 tbsp | Fresh Lime Juice | 2 tbsp |
| 4 tbsp | Simple Syrup (p. 99) | 4 tbsp |
| 6 ozs | Soda Water | 180 ml |
| | Ice Cubes | |
| | Lime Slices | |

In a tall glass, combine lime juice and simple syrup. Add ice cubes. Slowly pour in the soda water and stir gently. Decorate glass with lime slice. Serve immediately with a long straw.

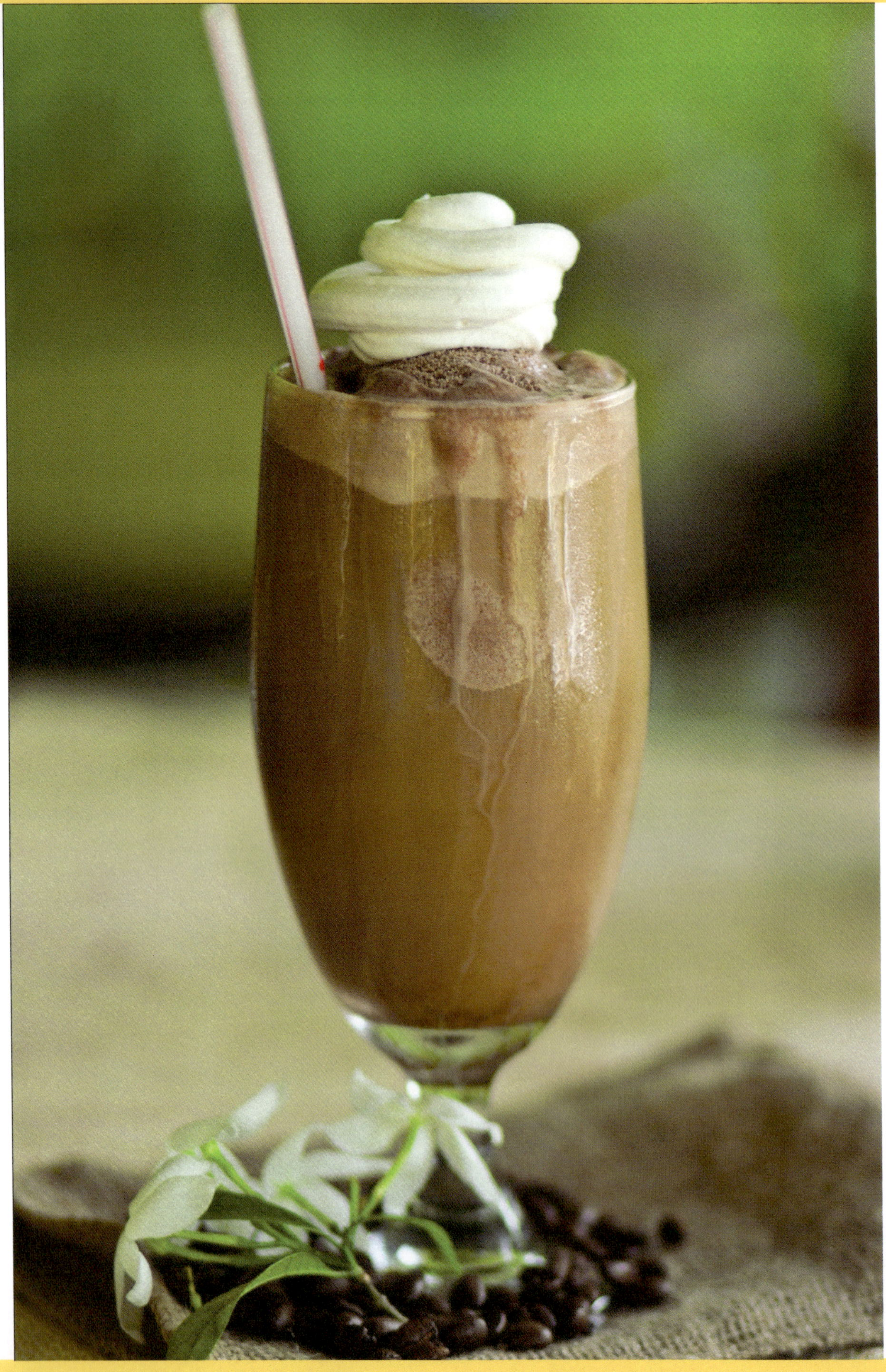

# PLANTERS PUNCH

| | | |
|---|---|---|
| 2 ozs | Simple Syrup (p. 99) | 60 ml |
| 4 ozs | Jamaica Red Rum | 120 ml |
| 8 ozs | Fruit Juice | 240 ml |
| | Orange slices | |
| | Marischino Cherries | |

Have 2 tall glasses ready and filled with ice cubes. Blend syrup, rum and juice well. Pour over ice cubes and decorate glasses with orange slices and maraschino cherries.

Choose orange, pineapple, grapefruit or mango juice or any combination of such.

DRINKS

# DAIQUIRI

| | | |
|---|---|---|
| 2 ozs | Jamaica Red Rum | 60 ml |
| 2 | Limes | 2 |
| 1 oz | Simple Syrup (p 99) | 1 oz |
| | Ice Cubes | |

Halve and juice limes. Strain. Add all ingredients to blender and beat till well combined. Pour into 2 short glasses and decorate with lime slices. Serve immediately.

Makes 2 drinks.

# SIMPLE SYRUP

| 2 cups | Granulated Sugar | 500 ml |
| 2 cups | Water | 500 ml |

In a heavy saucepan, combine sugar and water and place over medium heat. Bring to a boil, and simmer for 5 minutes. Remove from flame. Cool completely. Store in covered container in the refrigerator and use as needed. Syrup will keep for 5 months.

Yield: 1 quart/liter

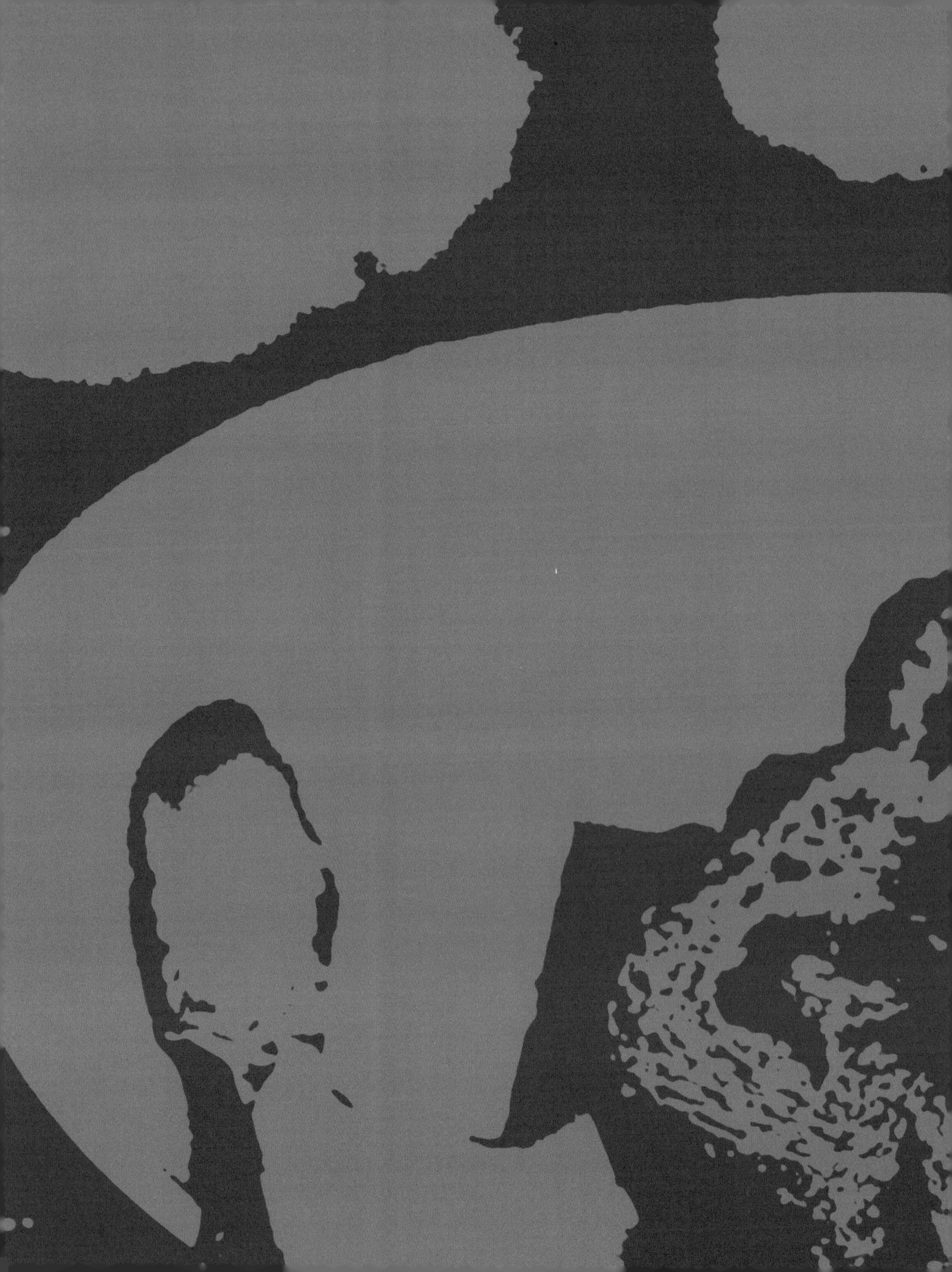

# JAMS JELLIES PRESERVES

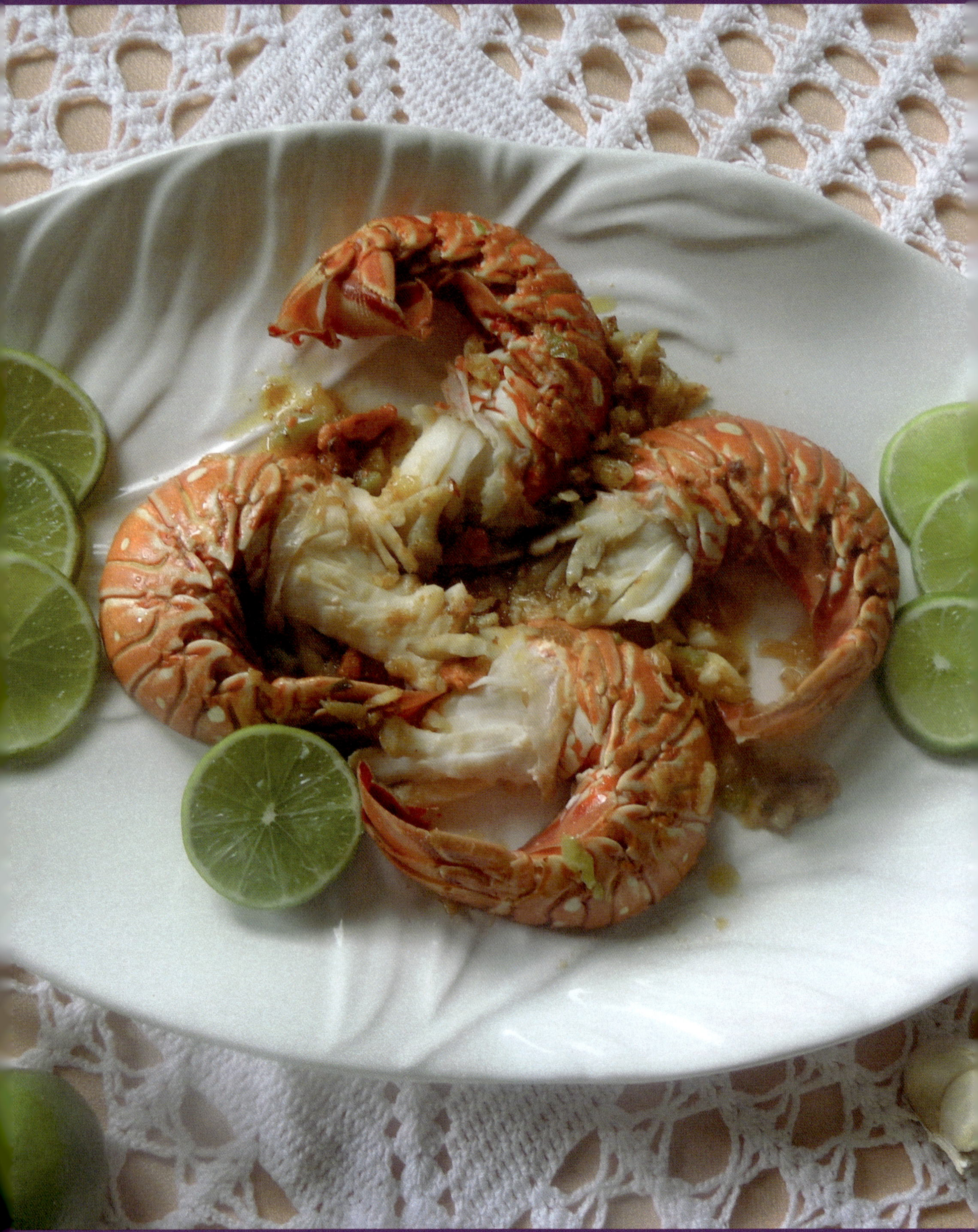

# OTAHEITI APPLE CHUTNEY

| | | |
|---|---|---|
| 6 cups | Otaheiti apple cubes | 1 ½ liters |
| 1 large | Onion | 1 large |
| 1 cup | White Vinegar | 240 ml |
| 1 cup | Granulated Sugar | 225 g |
| 2 ozs. | Gingerroot | 2 ozs. |
| 1 tbsp | Pimento Seeds | 1 tbsp |
| 1 large | Scotch Bonnet Pepper | 1 large |
| ½ cup | Raisins | 60 g |

Wash Otaheiti apples but do not peel. Halve and remove stems, seeds, and the bud ends. Dice into ½ "/1cm cubes. Peel and chop onion finely. Wash and peel ginger with a small, sharp knife. Grate and juice with about ½ cup/125 ml of water. Slice pepper in thin slivers.

Combine all ingredients along with 3 cups/750 ml water in a non-metallic or stainless steel Dutch pot (**do not use aluminium**). Place over medium heat, and cook to a gentle simmer, stirring often. As soon as apples are cooked through, about 20 minutes, remove from heat. Allow to cool in pot. When completely cool, spoon into clean glass jars making sure liquid covers apples and cap tightly.

Will keep for six months in cupboard, but refrigerate after opening.

Yield: 5 12-oz./375 ml. jars

# ORTANIQUE JELLY

| | | |
|---|---|---|
| 5 cups | Fresh Ortanique Juice | 1 l 250 ml |
| 5 cups | Granulated Sugar | 1 kg 225 g |
| 6 oz. bottle | Liquid Pectin | 200 ml bottle |

Cut ripe Ortanique in half and juice enough to make the 5 cups. Use only fruit in good condition with no bruises or soft spots.

In a heavy non-metallic or stainless steel pot, bring the juice and sugar to a vigourous boil stirring often. Boil for about 10 minutes. Add liquid pectin to mixture and oil for a further 10 minutes. Remove from heat and cool down somewhat. Pour into clean glass jars and cool completely. Cap tightly. Jelly will take about a day to "set" completely.

Makes about 6 12-oz. /375 ml jars

# SORREL PRESERVES

| | | |
|---|---|---|
| 4 cups | Sorrel Blossoms | 1 liter |
| 4 cups | Granulated Sugar | 1 kg |
| | Water | |
| 3-4 | Limes | 3-4 |
| 5-6 | Whole Cloves | 5-6 |

Wash sorrel thoroughly. Cut each blossom into slivers. In large ceramic or stainless steel pot combine sorrel, sugar and cloves and about a cup/250 ml of water. Cut limes in half and remove seeds. Juice and add to sorrel mixture. Bring to boil over high heat, then lower and simmer, covered for about 20 minutes. Remove from heat and take out cloves. Cool slightly and spoon into sterile glass jars. Cool completely and cap tightly.

Makes about 4 12-oz jars. Perfect accompaniment for roasted ham, turkey or pork.

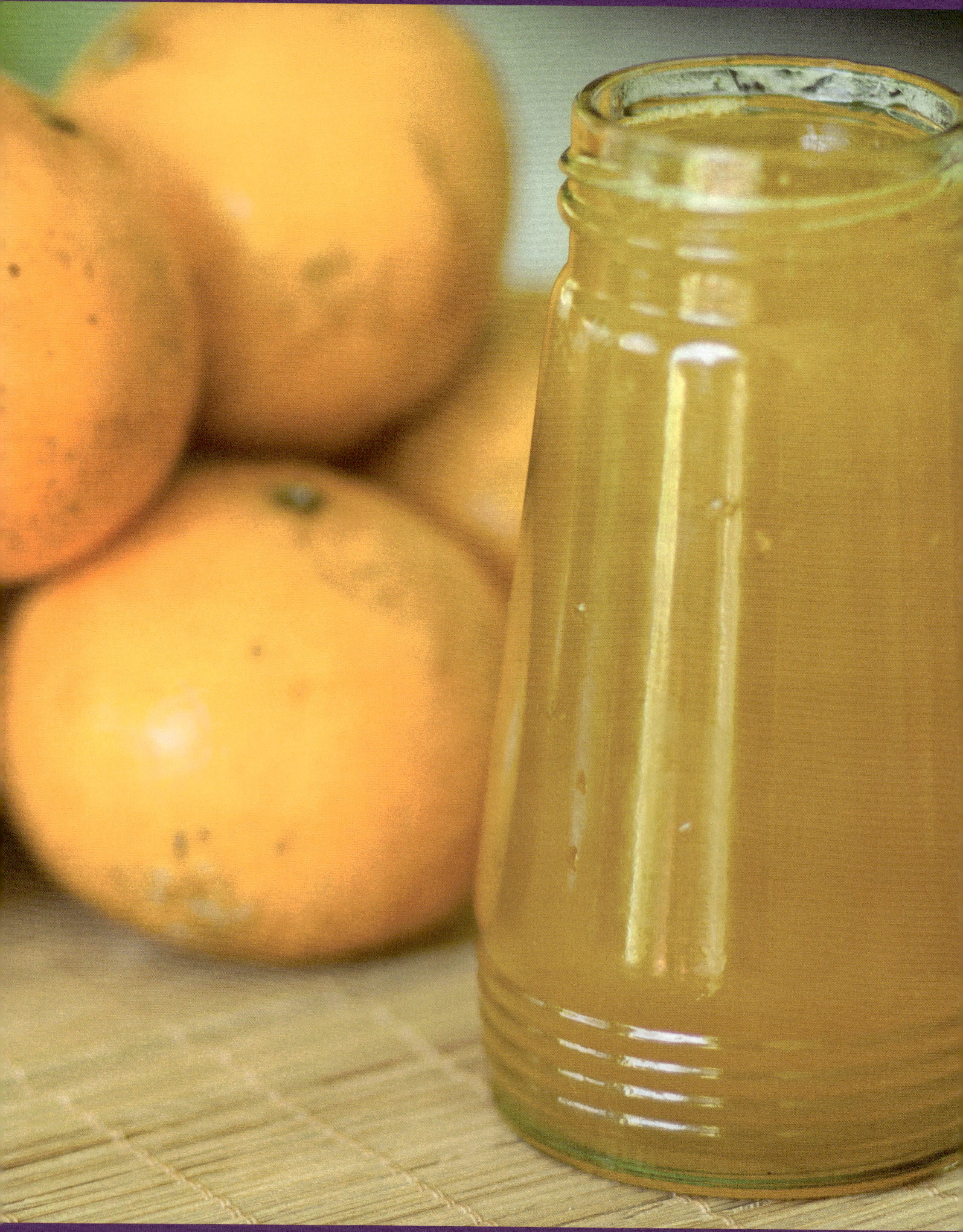

# JUNE PLUM JAM

| 12 | ripe June plums | 12 |
| | Granulated Sugar | |
| 6 oz pouch | Liquid Pectin | 200 ml pouch |

Wash plums thoroughly. Select ripe not **overripe**, unblemished fruit.

Peel and place in a large ceramic or stainless steel pot. **Do not use aluminium.** Add about 2 cups/500 ml of water, cover pot and bring to a boil. Lower heat and cook gently, stirring occasionally until the fruit falls off the thorny seeds and you can remove them. Measure the fruit pulp and add an equal amount of sugar to the mixture. Boil over medium heat for about 20 minutes and add liquid pectin stirring well and boil for another 10 minutes. Remove from heat and cool somewhat. Pour into sterile glass jars. Cool completely and cap tightly.

Makes about 6 12-oz jars.

JAMS JELLIES PRESERVES

# PINEAPPLE CHUTNEY

| | | |
|---|---|---|
| 1 | Pineapple (large) | 1 |
| 1 cup | Brown Sugar | 225 g |
| 1 cup | White Vinegar | 250 ml |
| 10-12 | Pimento Seeds | 10-12 |
| 4-5 | Cloves | 4-5 |
| 1 | Scotch Bonnet Pepper | 1 |
| 1 med | Onion | 1 med |
| ½ cup | Raisins | 125 ml |

Select a large, ripe pineapple with no brown or soft spots. Cut off the head and peel. Cut in quarters and remove the core. Cut quarters into small chunks. Cut pepper into thin slivers. Peel onion and chop finely. In medium ceramic or stainless steel, but not aluminium, pot combine all ingredients and bring to a boil. Reduce heat and simmer for about 20 minutes. Remove from heat and cool. Place in sterile glass jars. When completely cool cap tightly.

Makes about four 12-oz jars. Perfect with chicken and pork.

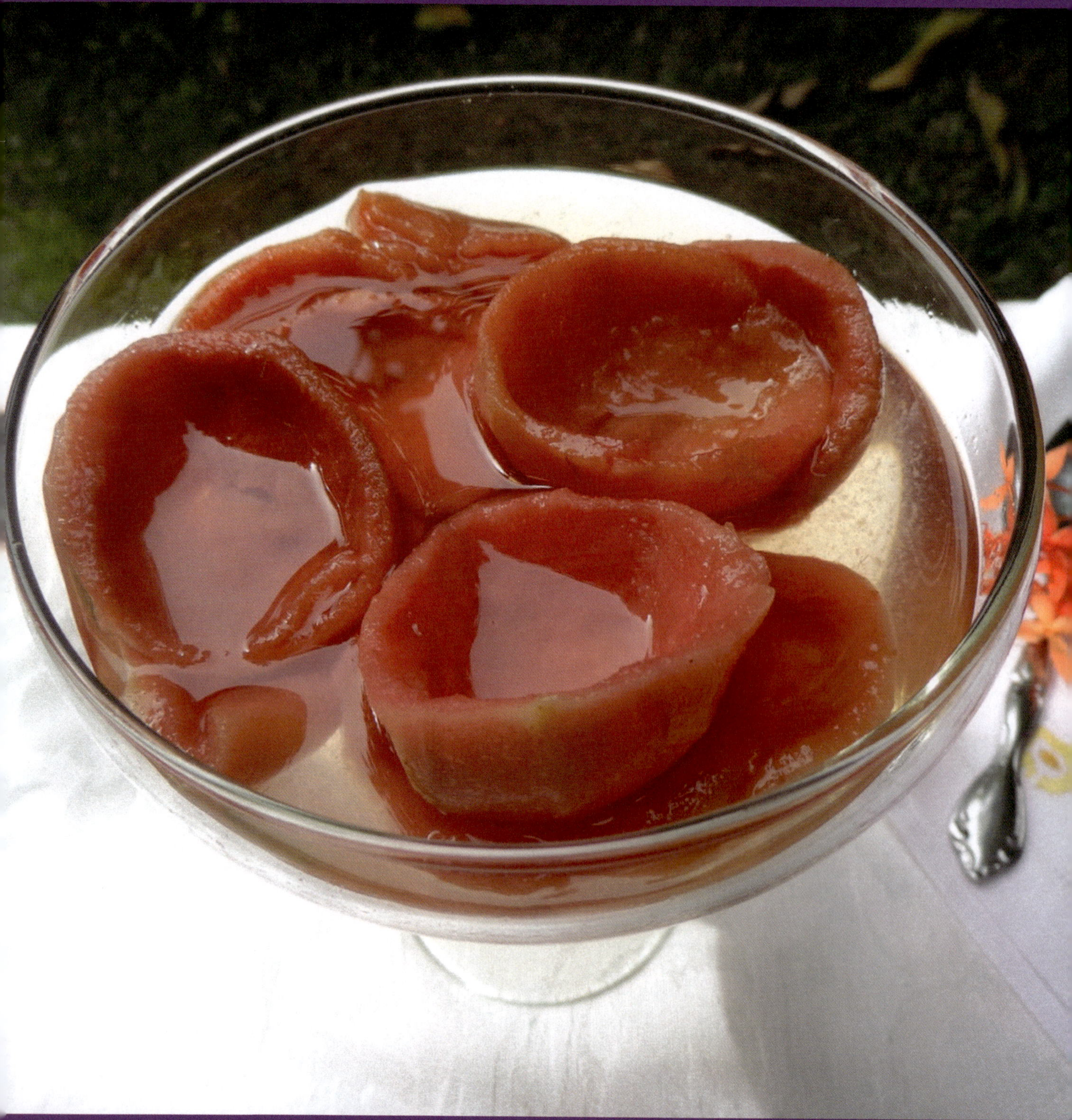

# STEWED GUAVAS

There is hardly any other fruit that can match the guava for the richness and depth of aroma and flavour.

| | | |
|---|---|---|
| 10-12 | Guavas(ripe) | 10-12 |
| 1 cup | Granulated Sugar | 225 g |
| 2-3 drops | Red Food Colouring(opt) | 2-3 |
| 3 tbsps | Cornstarch | 3 tbsps |
| | Water | |

Wash guavas. With a small, sharp knife peel the guavas thinly, then halve. Scoop out the seedy pulp. In a heavy medium-sized pot, combine the pulp with half of the sugar and about 1 cup/250ml water. Bring to a boil then lower heat. Stir occasionally. After about 15 minutes remove from heat. Cool. Put through a sieve, pressing down on pulp with the back of a large spoon. Discard seeds.

In sane pot, combine the shells, the pulp and the rest of the sugar and about 2 cups/500ml of water. Bring to a simmer, stirring occasionally and cook for about 15 minutes. Add the food colouring now, if desired. Dissolve cornstarch with a small amount of water and add to guavas. Allow to simmer for another minute or until liquid becomes clear. Remove from heat and allow to cool. Store covered in refrigerator.

Serve by itself or over ice cream or cake.

JAMS JELLIES PRESERVES

# ORANGE PEPPER JELLY

| | | |
|---|---|---|
| 4 cups | Fresh Orange Juice | 1 liter |
| 8 large | Scotch Bonnet Pepper | 8 large |
| 5 cups | Granulated Sugar | 2 kg |
| 6 oz. bottle | Pectin | 180 ml |

Wash and cut peppers into thin slivers making sure not to touch them with fingertips.

In medium heavy saucepan, combine orange juice, peppers and sugar. Bring to a boil, stirring occasionally. After about 10 minutes, add pectin, and continue boiling for about 15 minutes. Remove from heat and allow to cool. Pour into clean glass jars. When completely cooled, cap tightly.

Serve with roasted meats.

# ACKNOWLEDGEMENTS

Special thanks to

Coffee Industry Board
Banana Board of Jamaica
Coconut Board of Jamaica
Food Composition Tables compiled by Caribbean Food and Nutrition Institute
Christina Hosin
Mr and Mrs Arthur Thompson
All That Matters - Kingston, Jamaica


Additional Photography - William Greenwood

Printed in Germany
by Amazon Distribution
GmbH, Leipzig